This Tilting World

This Tilting World

Colette Fellous

Translated from French by Sophie Lewis

TWO LINES
PRESS

Originally published as: *Pièces détachées* by Colette Fellous
© 2017 Éditions Gallimard, Paris

Translation © 2019 by Sophie Lewis
Edited by Cécile Menon for Les Fugitives and published
simultaneously in the UK by Les Fugitives, London

Two Lines Press
582 Market Street, Suite 700, San Francisco, CA 94104
www.twolinespress.com

ISBN 978-1-931883-94-8
Ebook ISBN 978-1-931883-95-5

Library of Congress Cataloging-in-Publication Date
Names: Fellous, Colette, author. | Lewis, Sophie, translator.
Title: This Tilting World / by Colette Fellous ; translated by Sophie Lewis.
Other titles: Pièces détachées. English
Description: San Francisco, CA : Two Lines Press, [2019] | "Originally
published in French as Pièces détachées"--t.p. verso
Identifiers: LCCN 2019016022 | ISBN 9781931883948 (pbk.)
Subjects: LCSH: Fellous, Colette. | Authors, French--20th century--Biography
| Authors, French--21st century--Biography. | Jews--Tunisia--Biography.
Classification: LCC PQ2666.E47 Z46 2019 | DDC 848/.91403 [B] --dc23
LC record available at https://lccn.loc.gov/2019016022

Cover design by Gabriele Wilson
Cover photo by Candace Milon / Millennium Images, UK
Typeset by Sloane | Samuel

Printed in the United States of America

1 3 5 7 9 10 8 6 4 2

This project is supported in part by an award from
the National Endowment for the Arts.

For a long time, night after night, I welcomed it. It lived with me, loved me, enthralled me; I curled up inside my dream. And in the morning still I ached to sing out my joy. The scene: waves come crashing against the great bay window, the spray flies right over me but I laugh because I'm protected, I live in a house set right on the water's edge, perhaps even in the water, besides I see nothing of this house beyond the light of the glass wall, a vast light. It's very windy outside, you can see the wind dipping into the waves, playing with them. I'm not afraid, I am snug inside, right where I want my life to be, I'm looking at the sea, it's all I do, there's music in the room but you can't hear it, drowned out by the waves. For years I've summoned this same dream, the sea and its roar, night after night. On waking I'd say well, my lovely dream came back again, I would so like one day to find that house for real, then I'd say again, rolling over and reaching out: I shall walk through life until I find it, without seeking, perhaps it's already waiting for me? But where and when? I used to say that half jokingly, but still, I said it. A dream that seemed like an enchanted prince disguised as a house, a dream that brought me joy and made my eyes shine.

Now everything is clear, everything can begin, for this evening I am on the terrace of a house that looks a lot like the one in that dream, I've just made the connection between the light in each of them, I've just understood. The night is immense, superbly star-filled, the sea calm, still slightly violet, a border to the sky, it's as if I'm standing at the balcony of the world, of a vanished world. That's practically a line from before, I think, a line rooted in yesterday's world, but now it's over, my novel is damaged, the world is damaged, I too am deeply wounded, something has happened here, something real, but everything can still begin, everything can begin again, I firmly believe it, my heart believes, my eyes too. A white boat is gliding along the horizon, by the coast of Korbous, a tiny trembling point that shines in a straight line to Sicily, I half close my eyes to take it all in, it is Saturday and I love Saturday with a passion.

I must tell this before tomorrow, I must bear witness and right away, this book will be my nocturne, then I'll give back the keys and take my leave.

The phone rang, I heard the news and I collapsed. It was a Friday, two weeks ago, in the baking sun. I was down in the village buying a box of Safia water and raisins from Raf Raf, the ones that taste lusciously of roses. In front of the super- market, the fish-sellers were stacking slender sea bream on piles of ice, the yellow taxis were circling the roundabout, a man was selling Barbary figs out of his cart, from her seat beneath a tree a woman was hawking *tabouna* flatbreads from an old La Marsa basket, her hands tattooed with henna, she rearranged a shawl with big purple and yellow flowers on it around her face. I answered after two rings, I think people hurried to their balconies when they heard my cry, they wanted to help, but I picked myself up, I said it's nothing I'll be fine thank you. I always automatically say it will be fine even when it won't. I walked on down the alley, shaking, haggard, toward Avenue du 14 Janvier, utterly lost, I recognized the whine of the little train that goes to La Marsa, the one that almost ran me over a few years before. The heat muffled every sound, it was eleven in the morn- ing and already almost thirty-five degrees, days and nights of the country barely holding out against the relentless furnace. I glared at my phone, it had played a foul trick on me: it's my friend, in Greece, he was out on his boat, his heart, I've just found out, that's why I screamed, forgive me. That's what I wasn't able to say to the man who'd appeared bare-chested on his balcony and wanted to come down and help me: Alain has just, he's dead, I can't, forgive me.

Thank you, I whispered it in Arabic, very politely, and I added still in Arabic: Life be with you. All day long here we repeat life be with you, it's another way of saying thank you, we say it when we take our change, when we ask how are you, when answering someone's smile, when it's morning or when it's evening, when we're happy for someone else's fortune and we show it (then it's they who say it to us), life be with you; magical, protective words, a talisman, as if upon speaking it we sense that a mere breath could blow us away, there and then, and that talisman, the words that say life be with you, will ward off death, we say it automatically, without really thinking, then one day a life is blown away for good. Thank you, I said it three times, for my father always insisted that I never forget to say thank you. I know I say it far too much and that it often backfires but it's a habit, an old-fashioned way of holding on to him, of infusing all the lands around us with his presence, I mean that my father's face was his whole life, his life was the air he breathed, it was everything he saw and everything I saw with him, all the gestures we made to each other, all the looks we exchanged too, and our silences of course, and perhaps even what I didn't think to see when he was alive or that I couldn't see when I wasn't there. It was what I forgot to tell him and all that I forgot to ask him when there was still time. Yet my father didn't have any great educational principles, and I've no idea how my mother and he made ends meet while bringing up their five children, being themselves two urchins lost in the world, but those things, saying thank you, studying, honoring every moment, loving life, respecting others' lives, laughing, never giving trouble, giving joy, these mattered to him and he imparted them to us in simple ways, by laughing too, by the odd little affectionate tap on the thigh, by shyly twinkling his eyes to show that nothing was very serious really, that everything would turn out fine, or by shrugging awkwardly, playing the clown: that's life, that's how it is, you have to say thank you, it can't be helped. We used to watch him and laugh, we didn't know what to make of it: Was he teasing us or for real? At the very top of his back, on the left, there was a little knob of fat that fascinated me and bothered me a little too, he also had a few long, straight hairs on his shoulders, like head hairs, I couldn't look at those for long, I preferred to focus on his smile.

Now all that is over.

Lining the terrace, candles set in Sadika's amber-tinted glass vases make a kind of prayer. The night air, so mild in these parts.

I am calm just now, oddly calm and confident, in a country gone up in flames. Calm and incarcerated. Calm and damaged. The lighthouse's circling beam sweeps the sea, the cliffs, the great wrought-iron bays, and comes around again. The sea, the cliffs, the silence. On the last page of the book I wrote in this house, accompanied by the tireless circling of that beam, I remained silent before my own constant question. To stay or to leave? To go on or to stop? Until I wrote the last sentence, I didn't know if this book would close with my departure, I wanted it to decide for me. I would ask: Will I even be able to leave this house, to leave this country? Could this be the right moment, now, as the book is finished? But we could give no reply, the book and I. I reflected for a long time, then I gave up, I left the window open for the night to come in, with the obstinate dance of the lighthouse beam and Sadika's candleholder standing on the blue table, its friendly, forgiving flame, sweet Sadika, I put on music. "El Desierto." The voice of Lhasa, the low throb of the band, I gathered them close in my arms: the night, the song, the sea grown black and the few conspiring stars, I clasped them all very close, I shut my eyes, and this meant I would come back, it was a promise. Today is different. Tourists have been murdered, yesterday, on the beach of the Hotel Riu Imperial Marhaba, in the port of El Kantaoui. We have murdered our guests. Others died in the Bardo museum in March, all murdered. They disembarked at the port of La Goulette from their ships, the *Splendida* and the *Costa Fascinosa*, they took the cruise ships' standard Mediterranean tour (all the small crafts merchants know that Wednesday is a good day, the cruise ships' day is their best in the week, even those who speak only Arabic know the word for cruise ship), you'll have a grand day out seeing the old medina of Tunis, the ruins at Carthage, the glories of Sidi-Bou-Saïd, an eleven-o'clock tea with toasted almonds at the Café des Délices to admire the view of one of the world's loveliest bays and then, right after that, you'll visit the Bardo and see its marvelous mosaics. Our guests have been killed. Deaths on the Libyan border, for months now, others at Mount Chaambi, soldiers, policemen, servicemen. Militants for freedom murdered on the thresholds of their homes, Chokri Belaïd, Mohamed Brahimi. Tunisians have been killed. Bewilderment reigns in the streets, in all the faces, in the substance of the air, bewilderment and grief, the living body of our country has been wounded, its unique history disfigured. And now the whole country will be shunned by the rest of the world.

It all happened in the same period, over a few, short months. In Paris, the *Charlie Hebdo* massacre and the one at the Porte-de-Vincennes kosher supermarket in January.

The Bardo in March. Alain two weeks ago, and yesterday the beach at Sousse. Always on a Wednesday or a Friday. Of course Alain's death should not be on this list, it has nothing to do with the others, his was an accidental death, a heart attack, most likely. The others were murders, premeditated crimes, attacks. But these collective shocks, these blows to our bodies and our personal lives, have become interleaved with Alain's death, with the shock of that death, in the heat of the day, down in the village streets. He died on his sailboat, in mid-ocean, in the space of a few minutes.

I could talk about that death; I haven't the strength to discuss the others. This tilting world, how can we talk about it, make sense of it? Only by naming the appalling blow these deaths have dealt each one of us, the deep wound they have gouged that can never be healed, the birth of a new kind of warfare, and this terror that is taking root everywhere, even within our own bodies.

Yet through Alain's death, the violence of these assassinations reverberates, all the men and women whose lives have been torn out in a matter of seconds, in an office, a supermarket, stepping out of a bus, on a beach, a diffuse violence that watches and awaits us; but also the deaths of all those attempting to flee the terror in their own countries and who are drowning at sea, thousands and thousands of bodies tossed in this very Mediterranean Sea. As if his death, its happening almost concomitant to these many others, were an allegory for our times, for the world's metamorphosis and for the gradual disappearance of its previous incarnation, that world to which Alain, like so many others, had been committed from adolescence. A world in which the ambition, the dream, the utopia were to conceive and build our freedom and our independence, a world in thrall to creation, to art, beauty, pleasure, discovery, modernity, love, to the search for new forms of language and of expression. To compensate for the great distress that had characterized his childhood, that abandonment, he had chosen literature. Alain, Alain. I repeat his name softly while lighting the last candles. He used to like looking at the sea from this terrace, he would lean out to it, as if making sure it was all still there. He taught me how to find my bearings: there's Korbous, that's the island of Zembra and the smaller one, right beside it, is Zembretta. Over there's El Haouaria, where we went last summer, but you can't see it from here, and right on the horizon, can you see, that's the route to Palermo.

He had forged his passions for literature and travel into a total reality, he had raised them into his kingdom, a glorious delusion: it's words that create things, he would say, books created the world. Until the day he decided to stop writing, in 2009. At first the idea grew covertly inside him, a kind of emergency exit he could bolt to during the struggle to write a new book; at first he didn't tell anyone. To stop writing after creating an oeuvre focused on the search for a perfection he knew to be unattainable, only to be found in Antiquity, in mythology, or in the ancient eras he almost felt he had lived through. It was then, secretly, in the way we feel a fever gradually coming on or how we touch our forehead to check, not altogether sure of being ill, just a little shaky, a sense of weakness in the legs, that he began to doubt his powers and his books. He no longer believed in literature's utopia, he must have been aiming too high. Literature could no longer be his one and only god, it didn't work anymore, better to raise the white flag and give up: Maybe I've nothing more to say, that's what he wrote in his diary. He left literature as one leaves a country, as one goes into exile, as one abandons one's history. And by slow steps, he settled into silence. "Heart and soul," he emphasized in May 2012, just before his first time out on the yacht called to an alternative utopia: "I have withdrawn, alienated, walled myself inside my silence, since I refuse to allow one more book the right to force me to give it life. A deafening silence that gnaws at my body, that cuts me to the quick, but in which I'll persist, like a man gripping the guardrail with both hands as he gazes at the abyss into which he can't stop wanting to leap. My silence commits me to a voiceless struggle not only against this world of ours and all its noise, but also against all those writers who blithely go on believing in it."

The simple formula he'd found, the one meant to liberate him but that became a prison of his own making, was: "I write no more." The briefest of slim volumes, written a few weeks before January 11, 2011, as the social and political situation in Tunisia deteriorated, growing more rotten with each day. He was no longer sure he wanted to stay in this country: Why not move to Crete with Sadika, his beloved, his refuge; why not make a new life there? He wasn't sure, he hesitated. Tunisia was suffocating him, it no longer glowed with the light that had so enchanted him, everything had become so constricted, not enough space for writing, no, this wasn't the life he had dreamed of. He had even noted in his diary, presciently, that he feared his decision might herald a disaster to come, something of wider, more collective impact: "Sometimes I wonder if *I write no more* might not anticipate some fundamental collapse, some kind of disaster on a much greater scale." Going back to his words and to his voice now, right after the attack at Sousse, staring at them, touching them, to try to close in on their secret.

He died like a Greek hero, with an unheard howl, in the middle of the Aegean Sea, at the helm of his yacht, where he loved to be. He died "on the surface of the watery plain," as Théramène says in Racine's *Phèdre* when we come to his great account of Hippolyte's death. "On the Surface of the Watery Plain" was the title Alain had given his logbook, begun for his first Mediterranean crossing. For the book's epigraph, he had chosen a line from Plato: "Living, dead, or on the high seas." But the terrifying monster that rose from the water and killed Hippolyte in Théramène's tale was this time conceived within Alain's body, in his own heart. His life ended in the homeland of those he had loved and exalted, so we might imagine he had chosen this death, even without knowing or inviting it. He who was forever trying to recover a trace of the Greek gods, to follow the threads of mythology's great journeyers, to seek out the places where the prophets had wintered, to hark back to Odysseus's world as well as the Ancients', to check his readings of Plato or Thucydides, or to head off on the trail of Pythagoras, to the grotto on Mount Ida in Crete, to see with his own eyes whether the mouth of hell truly gaped right there. And he had with childlike jubilation found traces of Zeus, Cronos, and even of the she-goat Amaltheia: Look, it was to this cave that they came, he would say to Sadika, look, it really was right here. And his eyes would be shining. On each journey he would discover and rediscover, and he loved to write it all down, to transform it into fiction. For a few moments, he would become Orpheus, Odysseus, Virgil, Homer, Herodotus: the page he touched and covered in writing now became a shrine. But the decision to stop writing and to announce his cessation publicly tore a rift in him, sowed a distress much greater than he'd anticipated: we thought him swallowed by his own void. Like a reiteration of those childhood times he used to call "the dead years." By ceasing to live as he'd always lived, that is, sitting down at his desk every morning for forty years, always with a new book to write somewhere inside him, and above all, by announcing this, he had with one blow shattered his entire life and undermined his dreams. He spoke to no one of his distress, or only in a few words, punctuated by a shy, self-deprecating laugh. But his personal tragedy arose from his inability to back out: he had declared his retirement, he had to do it. In fact, he'd condemned himself. He still had his love for Sadika, the woman for whom he had dropped everything and with whom he was living in Tunisia, near the Gammarth Forest. Sadika and the force of his dreams, his desires, his untiring curiosity.

He also still had the sea, his newest love.

Yes, at some point the sea replaced his faith in literature, now he wanted to sail it up and down and traverse it as you do the chapters of a novel you're shaping from one day to the next, from page to page, from port to port, in the joy of advancing, of discovering, of being alone between the sky and the water, far from those who had thoughtlessly murdered his first passion. For Alain the Mediterranean had become the work to be lived, rather than written. Now and

then he seemed comforted by it but that was a façade, perhaps of pride, for how, at this point, could he ever go back?
To set sail, far from the towns, far from those who—as ever
according to him—had abandoned him, to cover kilometers,
slowly, to keep on going, not to feel his decision as a failure:
this would be his new endeavor. I was watching him describe the itinerary of his first voyage to me, I followed the
line of the red felt-tip across the map pinned to the wall in
the big dining room at Raoued, he was stoking his excitement by describing the research he'd done into the art and
science of navigation, he pushed out his chest for courage, to
prove he was happy, and I believed him, for of course he was.
I admired his capacity to discover a new world so quickly,
I congratulated him, a little surprised but happy, too, at the
sight of such passion.

He bought a single-masted yacht, the *Phocea*, named
after the Ancient Greek city in Asia Minor, on the Gulf
of Izmir. The name was not his choice but that of his for-
mer landlord, a very elegant man of seventy: I'm selling her
because I feel I'm no longer strong enough to steer, I'm beginning to grow old, it wouldn't be wise to go on, but it's a
wrench for me, the man had said. Alain went with Sadika
to France, to Aigues-Mortes, to collect the yacht. But everything I'm saying here troubles me because I'm implying
that his death was a suicide, a logical death brought on by
his break with literature, his reason for living. No—he died
brutally, in a moment of happiness, never realizing that it
was the end. A pause in time, nothing more. With the sea
all around. His last whispered words were: "We'll go on." He
didn't know these were his last words, he really meant the
yacht should continue on its course, not stop before the next

stage, that's what he'd decided, in this too he must not waver, they'd soon reach Santorini. There is something grandiose about his death, like a scene you could slot straight into a classical tragedy, with Théramène's parting words: "Forgive my grief. For me this picture spells / Eternal sorrow and perpetual tears."

At first I didn't recognize Baptiste's voice on the phone, I was blinded by the sun, I couldn't even see the number that appeared on my screen. The man selling the Barbary figs asked if I wanted to taste one, he peeled and held one out to me, it was beautifully golden, I smiled and showed him the telephone, not right now was what I meant. It's awful, awful, the voice repeated. Tears overlaid and broke up the words. I didn't understand, I didn't know who was talking, I don't think he would have recognized his own voice just then, it was so changed, so filled with pain. The heat suddenly became appalling, so dense that I saw only a deadly brightness, a brand-new plane of air, raised and set off-kilter by the horror of that voice. As if, just here, we had broken away from every moment that had gone before. I could no longer tell what was real from what wasn't, the light settled in drifts in the alleys, everything was turning too white, this white already dissolution, loss, blindness. Who are you, what's happening, I asked, I don't understand you. But it's me, Baptiste said, Alain is dead, it's awful, Alain is dead, I don't know what happened, I haven't even called Sadika yet, how can I tell her? He tried to answer my questions. He died in less than two minutes. With that, like Théramène, he began to tell me. We'd set off from Amorgos. He didn't seem at all tired. He just asked for a little water, which surprised me because he never usually drinks water after his morning coffee, I remember thinking that. He made some strange gargling sounds, I was on the other side of the yacht, I turned and saw him and for a moment I thought he was fooling around, trying out a nonsense language. But then his head fell against the rudder, his mouth was slightly twisted. Jacques and I thought he'd fainted, we told him, quickly, Alain, we're heading back to port, we have to turn around. We didn't know how to restart the motor ourselves, it was always Alain who steered and we were an hour from the shore. He didn't move, but I know he heard us because he distinctly said: No, no, we'll go on. Then he died. Those were his last words: We'll go on. It's awful, I can't believe it. Sorry, I have to hang up, they're calling me, we have to do some paperwork.

That is when I screamed, when I realized that it wasn't a joke and we really can die like that, in the middle of a sentence. Alain was dead, it wasn't a fainting spell, they hadn't been able to save him. Off the coast of Amorgos: its name suddenly island of love and death, both at once. He'd messaged when he arrived to say that the crossing from Patmos to Amorgos had been tiring but spectacular, that at last they'd reached the realm of *The Big Blue*, after two days of easy sailing. Amorgos marked one of the major steps of his voyage, he had spent the whole winter planning the yacht's route with minute and methodical care, sitting each morning at his desk as he used to do when he was still writing his novels. By the window with the jasmine. He would unfurl ancient maps over the couch along with encyclopedias, history books, and adventure stories all around, stacked up on the kilims. Then, for his third summer, he had embarked on a voyage meant to last two months. The Mediterranean had become his new life, his delight. We couldn't have dreamed it would bring his death.

He had plotted out each chapter, from Turkey all the way to Tunisia, no more than one or two days for each stage: Greece, Sicily, Malta, and finishing at the port of Hammamet, where he would leave the yacht for the winter. The last words scrawled in his log: "Friday, June 12, 07.10. Amorgos, destination Santorini." His navigation plan too stayed next to the books on my gray wooden table; he'd sent it to me so I could join them at some point, him and his crew: "Itinerary, should you ever…" was the email's heading. Marmaris, May 25, then Bodrum, Samos, Patmos, Amorgos, Santorini, Kea, the Corinth Canal, Patras, Corfu, Cortona, Riposto, Syracuse, Gozo, and finally Hammamet on July 24.

His face was calm, Baptiste said, I don't think he realized what was happening. His pulse had stopped, we tried to do some chest compressions but it was all over. The yacht had veered toward the coast, we hit rocks, we were lucky to escape without a hole, then we ended up drifting out again, we'd forgotten about the sea. He was there, alongside us, then suddenly he was dead, it was incomprehensible. We didn't even know how to restart the motor, we used to follow his orders but he was the only one who knew how to sail, he had to be the only captain on board, we would help as best we could, this time we couldn't get it to work, we'd completely forgotten how to do it. And all that never-ending sea around us, Alain dead in our arms, the boat was going by itself and we let it. The lifeboat only reached us an hour and a half later, the doctor from Amorgos came on a fishing boat with his bag, he registered the death, he said we couldn't have saved him, even if the lifeboat had come sooner we couldn't, his heart stopped, he said again and again, it can happen, you know, he's not the first to die like this, out at sea, the heart gives up; come, we have some paperwork to do now.

That was two weeks ago. A Friday.

And then the horror of Sousse, yesterday, at the beach. Another Friday.

I didn't know how to walk through the village just now, I looked down as I passed the pottery-sellers, they too don't know where to look. Couldn't even bring myself to buy my evening flowers from Toufik, his basket is still full, he's not sold a single jasmine, couldn't even joke about Vive La France, he who greets me every time I go by: So, cousin, how goes La France these days? This time, not a word, eyes lowered, just a nod. Yesterday a young man in black surf shorts and a black T-shirt came to the hotel beach and killed tourists, he'd hidden his gun inside a beach umbrella. On my beach, our beach, on every beach, for thirty-five minutes, he killed people. Thirty-eight people. The police arrived very late, when all the bodies were lifeless, it's incomprehensible.

All as one now, shocked and silent.

I took the high lane into town, I wanted to look at things one by one for the last time. The Hotel du Figuier, empty. The geraniums withered on the doorstep. The trash-cans ransacked by cats. The terraces cracked, the walls crumbling, some houses abandoned, others still pristine white.

The insolent beauty of the bougainvilleas, red and white tangled together, I briefly saw the colors of the Tunisian flag and walked a little faster. I was alone in the alleys, as if under curfew at high noon. The lamps of the mosque came on all at once and startled me. The pink sky, the sun's rays on the sea, above the terraces, the profile of Bou-Kornine opposite the parking lot, its almost Japanese lines, I allowed the word *cyclamen* to stay with me because in spring we still like to go there on Sundays to gather bouquets. The last swallows dipped and dived over the garden of Dar-Saïd, I nodded to the guard of the new villas slumped inside his hut, I dead-bolted myself inside, I took some long, slow breaths, opened the window, and came back to the sea.

The night, on that terrace, so close to Carthage, I observe slowly, without tiring: the sea is my memory, my raft. It guides me through all the times of my life, at the mercy of my gaze which fixes on one point, then another and another even further, heads out to a wave, catches it, and rides it in to shore, touches on that little grove of eucalyptus and wild olives that comes between the sea and the houses perched on the clifftop; its movement dizzies me and seeks to lose me in losing itself. All I need do to discover the form of my book, however, is follow my own gaze, which alone may hold its truth, the truth it burns to speak yet has never articulated. It may take many detours, I know, and deep trust.

I say all the times of my life for brevity, but it's not my life; first of all it's the life of this country, then the lives of those I've encountered fleetingly one day, in a taxi or a café, on the road, on the beach, in a train, in the countryside, in France, Tunisia, Egypt, Italy, it doesn't matter. People. The lives too of those I've imagined and whom I call friends or figures rather than characters. My father is one of these. I don't know him well, I have to invent him, even though I grew up with him in the house, although that didn't last so long. Then he became my friend, I tried to listen to him, to understand and help him, we were shy with each other, I didn't want to upset him, he respected my freedom, I respected his. One summer, on the beach at Cannes, we really talked, it was nine in the morning and the first time we had breakfast together, just the two of us. I was twenty-seven, he was very elegant, wearing a red Lacoste T-shirt and sunglasses, and when I kissed him I recognized his cologne: a burst of real joy suddenly at having a father. It was a kind of secret encounter, we'd slipped away in order to meet, like lovers, he said what he'd never been able to say till then, he entrusted his words to me because he knew I would keep them safe.

At the limit of my vision, on the far side of the sea, lie Palermo, Messina, Taormina, Syracuse, Catania. And the ancient sweetness of the summer that slips into the sounds and colors of the towns' names. The sweetness of all those fifteenths of August when the Madonna is paraded through the lanes of La Goulette, and people turn into the little avenue, in joyous procession, walking through bouquets of muddled odors, the figs, flat peaches, lemon-scented tanning oil, gasoline, sweat, and *bottarga*, the odd, obscene red bundles that look like small twin fetuses tightly swaddled in wax, the dried roes hang from the faded blue window bars, sometimes you see them nailed to the ceiling in the long corridors of fishermen's houses; the walls are greenish and the corridors very dark; they're never lit because of mosquitoes; people just set their cast-iron chairs out on the sidewalk and fan themselves, like that, with their newspapers; and the night goes on, night after night after night, and very quickly that makes a life.

The faces come mainly from Sicily and Andalusia, we can't tell them apart now, they're very similar, no doubt because

29

they live together and very simply in this little corner of Tunisia, but their histories are different, mine too. We think we live without history but it's History that created us, we just didn't notice. I say "we" for ease but that's not altogether right, my family has always kept a little distance from this "we," in spite of itself. In the evenings, the Sicilian handcarts go around the cafés, as they do in Catania, the spinning tops, the hard candies, sticks of licorice, cones of toasted linseeds. The almonds and pistachios, the fluorescent Hula-Hoops, the first of the light sticks that glow like rainbows: you want one for yourself and right now. Coolers hefted on their backs, the strawberry and lemon granita-sellers thread their way among the tables and hold out folded paper cups, they scarcely speak, they do everything with their hands and we understand them because we're used to it. Our parents speak to them in Arabic, we don't. That's how it is. Our parents were born into the language but French is our native tongue: I don't know who instilled such a love for this language in us but we are, indeed, in love with it. We know the strolling food-sellers well, we call them by their names and they too call us by our names. Sometimes we come upon them during the day, on the beach at Khereddine or at Kram in the early evening, near Alfred's, the ice cream parlor, just in front of the black-and-white Salambo billboard. Tahar, Moncef, Amor, Hamid, Ali. I stare at their knotty fingers and their calf muscles, I smile and notice that their skin color is suddenly offset by the little red and yellow lanterns hung among the trees and in the restaurants' porches, sending diagonal streaks of light over the streets. I take in this alternation of deep darkness and dancing colors, they're tiny and so vivid, these colors, that I still hold them fast in my eyes, they are what I seek, hearts beating in this little crush of years, beneath the trees, I am intoxicated.

The handcarts are Sicilian but the sweet-sellers aren't any-more, they're all Tunisian now, they respond to my smile and are slightly shy. The Sicilians have gone, leaving their recipes and their Madonna, and we've not left yet. In any case, we don't know what country we come from, we don't try to find out, our families have been living here for centuries, we talk about Livorno, Seville, Lisbon, we take life as it comes, we don't care a whit, we're here and one day we know we'll go to France, to the country of our native tongue, it's the land of our loves and our dreams, France is our horizon. And in any case, we are born to love so many lands, leaving them doesn't frighten us, we like laughing, studying, and dancing, you can do that anywhere. "One of these days," has become our refrain.

Now, suddenly, the night grows dark and solemn, like the Ravel piano concerto. Café Vert is the only one still open, the handcarts have vanished, the sweet-sellers know they won't sell any more, the children are tired, they sleep on their par-ents' laps, and I'm staying up, I like to stay and watch. Words eddy from face to face until late into the night, they're bea-cons, little flares of joy that illuminate these families that come to take the night air, it's still too hot in their houses so they stay here, talking about life. I look at them all, face by face, and something melancholy seems to envelop them, as if they were already refugees, hostages, or prisoners I should one day save, I don't know when, it's very muddled, I don't even know how many years a life can last, and so I say a very long time from now I'll save those people. And I say, too: Could all of us, perhaps, without knowing it, the French, the Italians, the Maltese, the Jews, the Greeks, the Muslims of this country, we who watch and play together at the café, in this small nowhere-town, yes could all of us already be refugees, already hostages or prisoners, or even disappeared? Or is it that evening unease plaguing my vision again? I'm seven years old, I rub my eyes, I can't yet tell anyone what I see, quite distinctly: the roar of annihilation. A breath of wind over the tables, over the terrace at Café Vert, and everything is gone, there's nothing left. This is what keeps me from sleeping, what chills my heart, but I never tell anyone my secret. I am among them without being of them, that's my secret, I don't want to join any group, I want to see life with my own eyes, I want to be free. I don't analyze my unease, I feel it and I grow up with it, I mean it grows with me, I can't leave it behind, even when I understand it better. Seven, eight, twelve, fifteen, seventeen years old, it's still there, it frightens me. It has no name but I know its source is a shadow that looms over us. I'd like to escape it, I'd like to be elsewhere. I'm not from here and I know that only by leaving will I save everything that lies before me now.

I look again at the mouths opening, closing, giggling, grimacing. There's lemonade, coffee, and sunflower seeds on the tables, the women are wearing flower-print dresses and the men starched white shirts, I'm a little sleepy but I must look very carefully, this is what I order myself to do, miming the words so as not to disturb my parents: look, look and listen to everything they say, keep looking. There are so many new scenes to discover and decipher: Why are the sellers and the waiters different from us and how are we different from them? Why am I not one of them? No one explains this to us, we can only be there and understand; my fabric is assigned, now I must sew the dress. So I twirl my neon light stick and with it I must peer again and again to draw sense out of the night's darkness. This moment is unique, like all the others, I refuse to drop a single crumb of my childhood hours, I dance my way around the tables, I circle them in a little ceremony for their protection, I want to keep them forever, even when I'm far away and have left them behind. I'm seven years old but this evening, in my dancing and quite alone, I've learned that life calls on me when I call on life, and only if I call.

Through those summers and on those beaches I grew up: at Khereddine, Salambo, Carthage, La Marsa, at Gammarth, Hammamet, Sousse, and Kelibia. There I learned to read this alien land, alien to the one where I thought I belonged, this land where we were in fact merely guests, though we only half realized it. Now and then it would appear, something touched us, an appalling story was referred to, then very quickly it vanished, our anxiety dispersed, and we could take up our lassos, our chants, and our Hula-Hoops again, stowing within us love for this country, inscribed for eternity in our very skin.

Burned, wrecked, violated memory.

The evening breeze blows into the house and with it the words of Roland Barthes, there, in volume IV of his

Complete Works, which I've laid on the table. It was March 1979 when he decided to give up his weekly column for *Le Nouvel Observateur*. His voice—I summon it once again— his voice gives me strength and I love it more and more, it's a voice I miss: calm, firm, sensible, lucid. His last column was titled "Pause" and in it he explained why he had chosen to write his columns in the curtailed form of the fragment, which was somewhat like haiku, and why this would be his last. "When my column appears, I am dismayed to see my little prose, my (studied) little syntax, in short my little form, crushed, as good as canceled by the overpowered writing that surrounds us. Yet we do have to fight for softness: From the moment it's deliberate, doesn't softness become a force? My writing small is a moral choice."

I try to find my way back to him as he wrote these words, to fill in the color of that moment: how he was dressed, per- haps a cigarette at his lips, a cologne, what cologne that day? His eyes squinting slightly—against the smoke? There is a struggle for softness. That evening I too, in my turn, I would like to bring those two words together, I'll take them for my shields and then this book can be my fight for softness.

It was he, there's no question, more than my parents, who taught me to read the world, to leave nothing in limbo. All things observed, all words spoken, every silence between two words, every link between two sentences. A wicked gleam in someone's eyes as they talk, or else a smile that breaks out and illuminates their entire face. The space between two people, the positioning of their bodies, sight lines, what's hidden in their gestures, in objects, in land- scapes. Political speeches, the shapes of cities, everyday con- versations, the violence that leaches into everything, bodies drawn to each other and then suddenly embracing. The potency of a single sentence, its reverberation down the years. How to give every detail a place of consequence and fresh value. How to work so that everything both connects and comes apart and we see it all anew. How to dig beneath first impressions, to discover a second language, to create hidden connections, associations, reminders, echoes, harmonies. To make everything more capacious and our lives unique.

"Una furtiva lagrima" pours from the computer onto the table, Pavarotti's voice drapes the whole room, it settles over the fabrics, the paintings, the plants, and carpets, it names them, one by one, and celebrates them. Following the line of his majestic, invisible voice, I take in each object for the last time. I salute each, one by one, joy comes into the house, *negli occhi suoi spuntò*, it flows in and brims at the eyes, mingles with the country's silent tears, this world, it's confirmed, I will leave tomorrow.

Tomorrow, yes, I will leave this house, I'll abandon the village and the life here, all the faces that I love I will leave. The friends, the objects, the doors, the sidewalk slabs, the tall eucalyptus and the wild olive trees, the orange groves, the roads, the markets, the music, the fruit, the dancing, my window of blue, I'll leave it all, no strength left. I don't know how I'll get to sleep. Just now I changed my bed around to try it out: With your head to the north you'll sleep better, Souad told me. You don't take enough care with your sleep, you don't take enough time for yourself. My answer is always the same: It's true, you're right. Souad loves to give me her little pieces of advice and I like to please her by listening, I kiss her and say again in any case she's always right.

Breathing close to her face, I recognize her sandalwood perfume, from Amarante, and of course, instantly, because it never leaves me, I recall that other scent, the one that lived in my parents' bedroom so long ago now, heliotrope, iris, and vanilla: L'heure bleue, a perfume imbued with the breath of the two people I've loved most dearly, two defenseless, unprotected souls. My father reads *France-Soir* in the bleach-white glow of the strip lighting, my mother embroiders a shoal of fish onto a linen sheet while listening to the *Moonlight Sonata*. It is she who perfumes the entire room, she is my queen. Much later that shoal of fish would drape the piano in her "little house" in Paris, and it has now come to me, to be stowed away in the Indian trunk; from time to time I shake it out, examine it, daydream, then put it away again, it smells very good. I follow the lines of the blue, yellow, and green threads that she meticulously interlinked, stitch upon stitch. In Paris she would play the sonata herself, on her Yamaha, every morning around ten o'clock, *adagio sostenuto*, I'd hear it through my bedroom window floating down from hers, a little higher up on the fourth floor, and tell myself it's a blessing because it means she's all right, she hasn't stayed in bed. Outside the house in Tunis, the avenue is deserted, you can hear the last tram rattling toward the Bardo. Only the Mobiloil garage sign and its handsome Pegasus, pulsing his colored lights over our balcony, still have some life in them. It's through those colors that I recapture the smell of the house. I ride among the colors as if on a flying carpet, they help me to see better, to travel among the years, the gardens, and the forgotten people. In my lap lies the navy-blue booklet of fables for reciting. I close my eyes, concentrate and, for the seventh time, I begin "The Ant and the Dove"; this time I have it by heart, I put the book back in my little red leather satchel, a kindness is never wasted, and it's my bedtime. On my parents' great bed the cats are already asleep on the open books, they play the bookmarks in our house and purr in their dreams. Now and then half opening a somnolent eye, they check that we're alive, then resume their top-secret adventures. They are part of the family and even share our nights when, with a questioning meow, they ask permission to slip beneath our covers and sleep curled up on our feet; no need for hot-water bottles on those nights, so each time naturally the door to our bed is opened, come on then, you, hop in. I count and recount, trek back through the years and the cities, I play hopscotch on our patio, shunting my Florent licorice tin all the way to heaven but I'm also the woman writing this book today in Paris, I allow Proust's voice to join me, "Everything revolved around me in the darkness: things, countries, years," and the voices of Flaubert, Maupassant, Rimbaud, I am never without their words for long. Maupassant had left Paris in 1889, after the world fair, he wanted to see new lands, new civilizations. He went traveling for a year—out of weariness, he said. He saw Florence, Sicily, Algeria, Tunisia. He wrote *The Wandering Life*. The book was published in 1890. At Maupassant's side I discovered the landscapes of Tunisia, his observations on the poor districts, the Jewish families, the new towns mid-construction, the early days of the French protectorate. He was surprised to find so many Jews in Tunis. I tally and re-tally the years: it was indeed on May 12, 1881, that the treaty of the French Protectorate was signed at the Bardo, at seven o'clock that evening. People called it the Bardo Treaty, and it was eight years later that Maupassant traveled through the country. Through his eyes, I saw it for the first time. To his views I mixed in my own errant years, those of my childhood, when I should have deciphered what appeared before me yet that remained a confusion. The French lycée; an unusual family; a Muslim country; the European quarter; Christian, Muslim, Jewish holidays: we celebrated them all together, we gave out festival foods on our doorsteps, but nothing more, I mustn't idealize. And Théodore

Roustan, Paul Cambon, the Regency, all those words dotted around the city telling the country's history, we didn't see them, busy as we were tasting the seasons' colors and all the sweet things. To us, they were just the names of an avenue, a school, a fashionable café. I mix up the years, I re-count three times, I convert the totals, I unearth vanished geographies and faraway sights, their echo makes me quiver, I say two million years, I say a hundred years, I say a minute, everything is far and right here, everything hangs around me and rots. These lives, these passers-by, these entwined bodies in low whitewashed rooms, these gardens running down to the sea, and the perfume that drifts from body to body in the afternoon and comes to rest at my forehead, I have never left them, even when I was far away. But I'm suddenly so afraid, again I see, over and over again, pictures of severed heads, bodies collapsing, some escaping down a side street, some who stumble and are slaughtered, some who were smiling or kissing the moment before they fall, I try to paint over their cries with older images, to shield myself: Roman ruins appear, olive groves, avenues happy on a Sunday afternoon, stepping out of the cinema, bouquets of roses filling the little kiosks opposite the great city theater. I pile everything together, to smother the sounds of gunshot. At every place, I restore the splendor of the light; that calms me. Then over again, everything begins to spin, I can't do it, I can't do it anymore. The violence has smothered everything. I want to return to the simple beat of that time when we used to breathe seaward with confidence, and the constant music that enveloped the streets and houses: Where have they gone, the songs of Feyrouz, Umm Kulthum, Hédi Jouini, and Abdel Wahab that used to fill the cafés and food stalls, mingling with the swallows' chittering and the copper-workers' hammering? I have a sudden urge to throw myself over the edge just as I threw myself off the great rock at Monastir, in front of the local kids, to show off, and to show that girls can dive too; I had launched myself from very high up, and it felt as though my fifteen-year-old heart floated completely free as I fell, ten meters high the rock was I think, and the kids, who could well now be the age of the Sousse terrorist's parents, the kids laughed and clapped. No, I've nothing left to lose, the powder-puff scent of the pink room will be my guide, I secure that scent with my words so as not to lose it, I dive with it, in it. The night is immense, the sea has suddenly turned an inscrutable blue, Alain is dead, I will not see him again, a life may end at any time, without warning, this is not new, but what to make of this violence, all those dead on the beach, all the dead everywhere, they are in me, haunting my lips and my eyes, no matter, I'll take this leap.

It's August in Tunisia, I come across this scene. Before the wrought-iron window frame, in full sunlight, you can come and see what's happening now as well as what has happened, you can sit and wait for the sounds to return, for the smells, the gestures, the words to revive and it's suddenly all so close to now. With patience and care you can return to every point in time. You go closer, you stare. A woman is there before the window, I recognize her. She is holding her father in her arms, it's strange because her father is still just a baby, his playsuit is baby blue and he's looking at her, it seems he too recognizes her, she is indeed his future daughter, his only daughter: his wild one, as he will call her. And she is seeking his smile, she calls him very softly by his name, Henry, Henry, she bursts into giggles because she's never before met a baby called Henry, she tosses her head and her hair back and talks while rocking him, tells him what has become of her and of the world since his death, in November 1982, in Paris in his black Peugeot that was almost his home, he loved it so much, this scene keeps coming back to her over and over, but she's never in the same place, it reappears unheralded, out of the blue. She was thirty-two and he seventy-three, she cannot forget, she asks if he remembers, she says he might remember if he pays close attention, because now you can come and go in time as you like, everything is possible, even never dying is an option, the evidence, here you are, *Papa*, and you're just a baby, yet you're my father and you died in November 1982, so do you remember that day, near the Quai de la Loire, do you?

Her father's heart had given way, yes, quite as cruelly as Alain's and doubtless just as her own would soon give way without warning, she shrugs awkwardly as he so often did and, echoing him, she says: That's life, that's how it is, it can't be helped. That day he'd wanted to carry out the big TV and put it in the trunk of his car. His son had given it to him, the one he called "my son the doctor": as his son had bought a newer, less bulky model, he'd said *Papa*, you can have the TV if you want it. Here are the keys, come and pick it up when you like. With great effort, he managed to heft it off the ground, first he got it into the elevator, his lips in a tight grimace, then he had crossed the shared gardens cradling it in his arms like a baby, people don't think of it now but they were very, very heavy, TVs back then, her dad walked like that, a little bent and very focused, all the way to the car which was parked a little farther down the alley. He managed to wedge it between two cardboard boxes, then closed the trunk firmly, exhausted but glad to have managed the task by himself, he wouldn't have dared to ask for help for he never wanted to bother anyone: See, I managed, all by myself, uff. And just then, he put his hand to his heart because suddenly everything seized up, he recognized the pain, unmistakable, piercing, precisely the same as two years before, when he'd been taken by ambulance from Château Pierrefonds, his nursing home, straight to intensive care at the Hôpital Tenon, but in this narrow street near the Quai de la Loire on the seventh day of November in 1982, there was no one around at this hour of the afternoon. He thought that if he rested for a moment it would pass, so he sat down at the wheel of his Peugeot to catch his breath, he didn't even have time to bring his left leg into the car, his strength gone, he died right there, in a Parisian backstreet near the Quai de la Loire, at around four in the afternoon, all alone, his car door open and one leg still on the sidewalk. A black Peugeot, it should be emphasized, for that car was his life, as he used to say. And in the trunk, the huge black TV, abandoned, already holding the seeds of images of today's world, invisible still but present, even those of November 13, 2015, were hidden inside it, with the faces of the hundred and thirty lives cut short and a photo of the killers, even those of the San Bernardino shooting at an office Christmas party, even those stupid local news items like the man in Florida who jumped into a lake to escape the police and was eaten by an alligator, and the story of the mouse that caused a stampede in a Moroccan mosque. The TV accepts all images, it deals wholesale, that's what it's for, but now it's fallen completely silent, in the trunk of the black Peugeot, silent and withdrawn, like the heart of the man who carried it. Her father's heart had given up. His heart that is also her own heart, she who is always at the window, in another time, at the very beginning of the twentieth century, with her baby father in her arms.

She's wearing a white dress with a black tulle flounce that brushes her knee, a very pretty dress.

I draw closer to the window to see her better. I recognize this woman: she is me.

Me in this book, attempting, in piecemeal fashion, to tell the story of a father born and dead in the twentieth century, and the story of this world now, this Tunisian village I shall have to leave behind, in this year 2015, a terrifying year, remorseless, in its new, twenty-first-century colors. More than a hundred years later. Even if leaving tears me apart, even if leaving destroys me, I cannot do anything else; Alain's death may have precipitated things. "It was his heart," the coroner said. The same sentence for Alain and for my father.

It's been ten days now of Alain's repose close to a tree in Gammarth. Jean-Claude and Sadika planted a papyrus on the grave, he used to love that little wood beside the sea. Now we must leave him in peace.

It's August of 1909, I am holding my baby father in my arms, he is seven months old, this scene is now in the book, I won't force it out. I need to stay there, to take up the story again, the whole story of my father, to see him close up, in a time I never knew. That summer, Proust began to write *In Search of Lost Time*, he turned thirty-eight on July 10, his father had died in 1903, his mother in 1905, from now on he could devote himself to writing his impossible book, he shut himself away and began. And that summer he made notes in the little diary that ran from January to March 1906, bought on rue Auber from the English jeweler Kirby, Beard & Co, the letters are printed in gold. Its dimensions are tiny, 10 cm by 6 cm. He left it untouched for three years and then suddenly he filled it. With notes, lists of names, a little sketch of Combray, the writing swings between microscopic pen-work and more generous penciled sections. He would copy these notes into his notebooks, then elaborate on them in his novel, where he would transform, refine, perfect them. I am wearing a white percale dress with a pale gray rose pinned at the neck and a black tulle flounce above the knee. My father gave it to me for my sixteenth birthday, we chose it together at Maison Modèle, it came from Paris and, as we left the shop, walking out in front of the great theater, we were both proud of this present. We held hands, a gesture sealing our love. It's always he who chooses my dresses, he always spots the newest styles, the black-and-white waxed jacket from Courrèges, the Françoise Hardy coat, or when I was younger, the cotton Carabi dresses with smocking or flowers or squares or straps or balloon sleeves. I'm always seeking his smile. He looks hard at me, as if he were fixing my eyes within his and so recognizing me; draw closer, he seems to say. Babies understand everything and much better than later on, when they're grown-up and know how to talk, to work, to seduce, lie, calculate, love, drink, navigate, go to war, and all the rest of it.

The swallows squabble and zigzag in the sky, a scent of aniseed, honey, and orange flowers drifts from the kitchen, a feast is in preparation, as usual, for it is Saturday, the holy day that brings with it a unique, majestic, unforgettable smell, unchanged for centuries. The sounds and smells of the house are unmistakable as ever, it must have been exactly the same a thousand, three hundred years ago.

My father's eyes are so black, so quick, so peaceable, and so confident that they make me want to cry. I ask him once more: Can you explain for me, please, how we've come to this?

He continues to gaze at me, it's clear he hasn't understood my question, for him my words are still just a noise among other noises, he greets faces, objects, tastes, and words just the same, his world is all of a piece, he makes no distinction between his own breathing and that outside his body, a long task lies ahead of him and I urge him to do it well, every hour is unhurried time for him and I see he's making rapid progress. He doesn't understand my question, his eyes are waiting for me to speak again.

I give him an extra little squeeze and he startles.

I should like to describe the *Charlie Hebdo* slaughter for him, the hostage-taking at Porte-de-Vincennes, the mass of people in Paris on January 11, 2015, the videos of beheadings, the orange coveralls, the anoraks, the seven-year-old girl and her explosive belt, she killed seven people, that was in Nigeria, and of course she couldn't understand she was going to die, they ordered her death remotely, by telephone. The Bardo museum and the murdered tourists, the first gunshots I ever heard in the video taken by a woman who was listening to the history of the mosaics, the one of Odysseus bound to his ship's mast so he can't succumb to the sirens, the one of the huntress Athena and the one of Poseidon, you can see heads turn as shots tear through the palace, faces fixed like in the mosaics, time freezes, and on the CCTV video, the killers walk through the museum's empty halls, they aren't in a hurry. But there are so many things I'd like to tell my father, the images stream past, I can't catch hold of every one. The recording of the black box retrieved in the Alps, when the copilot killed himself by smashing his plane into a mountain and all the passengers died, atomized, we could hear him breathing up to the moment the plane struck the mountain, his breathing is recorded, we retrieved it with the black box, threaded into the screams of all the others, behind him, when they realized that the plane was crashing. The earthquake near Kathmandu. Palmyra. The chaos in Libya. The volunteers signing up to fight in Syria, and this terror that encroaches and makes its home everywhere, step by step. The threats, the manipulations, the murders, the claims and counter-claims, the suicide bombers, the shootings, the attacks, I see it all happening at once, the beach at Sousse, the Bataclan massacre, the people killed at the Belle Equipe, Carillon, and Petit Cambodge restaurants in Paris, the triggers of this brand-new war, times and places in red and black telescope at top speed, it's like a B movie, badly shot, overstuffed with poorly connected plot twists and out-of-control violence, the shepherd decapitated at Sidi Bouzid, the suicide bomber and the bombed-out bus full of the president's palace guards, I would even like to say to him words that haven't yet been thought, those that will describe other bombings, other crimes, other fires, Bamako, Ouagadougou, everywhere is afflicted, we can't stop anything now. Tell me, please, how have we come to this? Only this very last sentence do I whisper in his ear.

I talk very softly so as not to upset him, he's only seven months old, I say it again. I say that I can't sleep anymore, that there are many of us who can't live with the violence any longer. Dismembered bodies invade my bedroom, slip away, and reappear like the nighttime beams of the Sidi-Bou-Saïd lighthouse on our terrace, I'm feverish, my life is parts and pieces, it consists of all these deaths, I must rebuild it to see it better, no one could have foreseen that our world would be so transformed, I'm begging: Help me, it's so you can help me that I'm writing this book. See how even at this point, in 1909, in Paris in the height of summer, Proust allows forgotten years, gardens, and faces freely to enter and people his book. See too how, in your house, other sounds enter and alight on the bars of your crib, swallows, the songs of summer weddings, the buzz of cooking, the clatter of the pony traps, the sound of the children's ball as they play in the alley, the piano upstairs, the call of the tomato-seller going by with his cart, the whole little world that's so alive around you. You know that when someone dies, a piece of your own life goes with them and the sounds that surrounded them go too, I am nothing without all the rest, this is what you used to tell me, what you passed on to me; in any case, it's what I have learned, so answer me now, it's your turn to speak. I laugh as I murmur those last words into his ear for I haven't forgotten that I'm talking to a baby and what I'm saying is ridiculous: Still, you could have warned me.

He looks at me and wrinkles his nose: Warned you about what? A fly has just landed on his eyelid, I brush it away.

About barbarity and human chaos, about ugliness. About madness, the unforeseeable, deception, betrayal, brutality. You told us nothing of this, never a thing, not a word even about the camps, you didn't want to hurt or frighten us, but your innocence—that too you passed on to us, and now we too are trapped, without arms or protection.

This father I'm holding, this baby in my arms, would later become my father. I think I put myself in my grandmother's place so I could talk to him and come a little closer to their story. She, my *nonna*, I have stationed in the garden behind the palm, she's sorting dried peas and lentils in a great bowl of water, she has her back to us, she's singing to herself. Snatches of Arabic, snatches of Italian. She is wearing a long red dress with loose pants beneath, it's the first time she's trusted me with her baby, she's taught me how to hold him. I'm not able to see her face, she's looking down, but for the first time I hear her voice. She is young and singing a little louder now. Her long amber necklace sets off her throat, displaying the whiteness of skin she never exposes to the sun. This one's an Italian song. Her native tongue is Ladino but she almost always sings in Italian, the language of her grandparents. I notice a little good-luck charm hanging from her necklace, a very shallow, well-sealed silver box containing sacred letters that we may never read but that must be carried around at all times, a kind of secret garment. It is secured or opened with a miniature gilded pin, and the children find it deeply mysterious because it has no explanation, we talk of the invisible and the unsayable but that means nothing to anyone, all we can do is look at it. Her husband is elsewhere, at work, on the other side of the city, in his little shop in the jewelry souk; I don't know the year he was born, I never asked any questions and now it's too late, everything's gone.

I only met my grandmother six or seven times, when I was maybe four, five, six years old. She would take turns staying with her children, a week with David, one with Robert, one with Gaston, one with Lucie, and then with us, in that house set in the heart of the city, right next to the great synagogue; she came only very rarely because we couldn't offer her a room to herself and my mother had nothing to say to her—how could she chat to her about Lady Chatterley or David Niven? She used to sleep on the living room sofa, never ate at the table with us and, during the day, she would sit in silence on the red leather armchair by the balcony. She would watch us go by, laughing and tussling, she was always impassive, we came to feel that she wasn't really there. For a long time I thought my grandmother was mute, and wasn't interested in us, that she was observing us from far away, as if we were foreigners and she foreign to us. I never went up to talk to her or kiss her, we didn't speak the same language, we called her *nonna*, that's all that she retained of her ancestors, one word, perhaps also a few recipes and some outlandish expressions such as *perdi zemane*, a mixture of Italian and Hebrew that she must have taught my father. He used to mutter these words under his breath, to himself, when he felt he was wasting his time with us or when he argued with our mother. My *nonna* wore a flower-print headscarf over her henna-dyed hair, I can see nothing of her beyond that headscarf, her silent gaze, and the red armchair. Occasionally a sigh. I was a little scared of her. Only my father would go and talk to her, he would bring her couscous with pomegranate seeds, a glass of tea, pistachios, almond biscuits, his gestures as if providing for a mendicant, I used to think, I didn't know what a grandmother was.

He was a loving father and son, as they say, but so delicate, so helpless, so disarming, even when he used to tell us he was a lion and we should be brave just like him. I watch him say it. He claps himself on the chest and throws his shoulders back, then, laughing, before our wide-eyed faces he repeats I'm a lion, I am, all my life I've been a lion. He cracks his head against the wall when he can no longer sustain the lion and it makes a dull thud that I can never forget, it's a scene that revisits me regularly and I won't rub it out because it's crucial, he does this several times, bashes his head before our stunned little shapes, he says he is ruined, he's got no way of paying his debts, we are finished, we can't go on. We bite our lips so as not to cry, we want to show that we're brave like him, so we stay there, we're loyal, we share in his distress. His head just catches the edge of the Cézanne painting hanging on the patio wall, it's *The Card Players*. He doesn't care if something happens to the painting because it was my mother's choice, she hung it opposite Van Gogh's *Bohemians*, to bring a French feel to the house. I fix my gaze on the frowning faces of the two card players to stop myself from crying, I've written that already too, I'm trying not to look directly at my father, the sound of his head hitting the wall frightens me horribly, there will be blood, he's going to die in front of us and without him how will we survive, he's gone completely mad, he's right, this time we're really finished, my mother will never be able to care for us by herself, all she loves is her piano, her books, and her romantic dreams, I will have to be a mother to her and I don't know if I'll manage, I'm too small to shoulder the burden of her story. But suddenly it's over, and quickly, my father goes to wash his face, he dries off with the white towel, his breathing returns to normal. And we all sit down to eat as if nothing had happened. The thing is incomprehensible to the six-year-old child I am. We eat the carrot, zucchini, and tomato ragout, we say it's very good, and we smile hesitantly at each other, we wipe our mouths with the white damask napkins, we're not very hungry, we don't want more, thank you, we push away the plate with its gold-painted rim. A separate smile for each person, we don't leave anyone out, we go right around the table, my father indicates with a hint of a twinkle in my direction that he's better now, that he's calmed down, and I can go to sleep without fear, everything will be fine, my wild one, don't be worried. Gradually I grow used to this family, I become part of it, there's nothing else I can do, I have to. Another day, perhaps the next day, he pops up in the same room, his arms filled with oranges, bergamots, fresh dates, and Saint-Honoré pastries from the *patissier* Gervais, his face is lit with a naïve glow, he laughs and hugs us, dancing us around him because he's done a fantastic deal with a French farmer from Béja, he's sold him the big yellow McCormick combine harvester and now, children, we're saved, we've no problems at all, we could even go right around the world, he flies me around in his arms, my head nearly touches the ceiling and I make myself laugh with him, now I can't stop, a kind of hiccuping, I hug him with all my small strength, you're a lion, *Papa*, hooray. When he gets home very late in the evening and I'm waiting for him on the balcony (I don't yet know that he first spends the early evening with another woman who isn't my mother, and this since I was born, I only found out by accident ten years later, in Paris), looking for him in the yellow head-lights of every car until I'm dazzled, I think that this man coming home much too late is not my father, this man who neglects us, who hardly says a word to my mother when he tosses a packet of Laurens cigarettes to her, he hasn't for-gotten to bring them, you see, Bice, I was thinking of you, he busies himself in the kitchen to make up for his lateness, come now, quickly, let's eat, children, it's ready. Rolling his *r*, he repeats it's ready, come now, children. Double-dealing, a double life. My true father has been murdered and I am holding back tears, this actor has stepped in so that we don't notice the difference. I'm quite sure of my interpretation and now I'm lying in wait for this impostor, this criminal. My fa-ther has been stolen from me, he's been killed or kidnapped, perhaps he's been thrown into the lake with the flamingos or into the Medjerda River, in exchange they've given me this replacement father who's working hard to replicate his gestures and channel his voice perfectly. My heart is beating so fast, I want to go out on the balcony and shout for help, come and save me from this con man, but no, above all we mustn't say a word, mustn't cry, we must keep the secret.

I smile. I smile at this man and squirm a little, I pretend that I've not noticed anything but he hasn't conned me, this is not my real father. I'm seven now, my grandmother died a year ago in March, just as the country won independence; she never knew the Republic of Tunisia, celebrated with red and white all through the city; she died on a Sunday, I saw my father weep that day, discreetly, while washing his hands, but I have not forgotten, our eyes met, I didn't know how to help him, he gave me a little pat on the head, he was so alone. I go on looking at this strange father who I can't trust anymore. A professional actor has made a minute study of all the gestures and faces my real father used to make, he's learned to imitate his voice; now he lives in our house, he touches our arms, tousles our hair, prepares meals for us. I have seen through his trickery and I remain on the lookout for that brief moment when his mask will slip, then, wham, I'll have him, he'll be caught, high and dry. I'll frog march him into the kitchen, down the hall, into the bedroom, I'll inspect his hands, how he makes his tomato sauce and the parsley stuffing for his *brik* pastries, how he brushes his teeth, hums, helps with our homework, checks our bookbags, folds our pajamas, puts us to bed, sets the water glass there on the side, don't read too long, you'll hurt your eyes. How he stands in for my mother who has retreated to her smoky bedroom and has been crying for a month at least, but we've gotten used to it, our mother is a part-time mother, in a few days she'll be better, we won't make a fuss, she's still the one we love best, our queen.

My father does everything in the house, this man has understood that much. I am stunned by how closely his movements resemble my father's, I watch him till I'm practically asleep, I admire his talent—then suddenly, I have to drop my neat interpretation, can't resist anymore, I whisper I love you in his ear and hug him very tight, night night, *Papa*, see you in the morning, why did you come home so late, we were frightened, you know, frightened of an accident, there were lots of cars and it was never you. All the same, my story had detected a lie that was hidden in his face and voice just then, but I couldn't prove anything, I was too young.

He plays all the roles in the household: father, mother, and friend. Never any reprimands, nothing off-limits, we have to find our constraints outside the house, we seek a balance between the world outside and that within, we begin to understand the geometry of our space and apply it to our feelings: freedom and kindness within, strictness and rules outside, together these form an inner mandala, gradually we add more circles and lines that cross over, repeat, connect, reinforce, we add colors, we find the pleasure in this life. He takes us to see the latest American musical comedies and all the Charlie Chaplin films, he buys us books, music, clothes, he teaches us extravagance, to laugh at the slightest thing, to demand that life be always more beautiful; he surrounds us with treats while sacrificing himself, he never chooses for himself, never has a preference, he makes do with what comes to him and, discreetly, watches over all that comes to us. He believes in luck, grace, and elegance, in liberty and modernity; he hopes for greatness for his children and makes no distinction between the boys and the girl, he tells her again and again he believes in her, she will find her own way, he's only a little nervous when she leaves for Paris, by herself: at seventeen, it's risky for a girl alone in the city, take good care. This is what he tells her in every one of his letters, take care because you are everything to me, he writes these last words in big characters at the bottom of the page and underlines them three times. His writing is fluid, generous, the blue ink has not faded.

He believes in all that's modern but he hardly knows what century he's living in, what matters for him is his children's future, his own life doesn't count, he seeks invisibility for himself, the word *future* is the one most frequently heard in this house and it happens to be the name of the ship that would carry me to France for the first time in June 1967, a brand-new ship whose maiden voyage I would share.

He wants to spare his children injustice and hatred, he pushes them toward France, he'd like them to strive to grace its shores and to grace other people's lives too because it was France, he said, that raised him out of dependency and injustice, we must be grateful to France. Make your own way, children, but be sure to make everything greater and more beautiful around you, each day greater and more beautiful than the last, never forget this, it's what I'm fighting for, for you my doctor, you my teacher, you my artist, you my dancer.

I, a dancer?

Yes, or an actress, whichever you prefer.

He often pats my thigh, a shorthand to demonstrate our personal understanding, each time I'm surprised and annoyed by this gesture, why always my thigh, I wonder, now I'm bigger I don't much like these teenage-boy moves, although he's my father he's still a boy. He tells me not to worry when I get back from school and they've just shown *Night and Fog* at the Tuesday film club. I'm thirteen, I want to describe the horror of the images to him but I can't do it, I only remember two or three, the heaps of hair, the shoes all mixed up, the rows of men and women, their eyes glazed, their bodies naked and so thin, but also the hypnotic railway tracks, the freezing cold that permeates the black and white of these shattered lives. I recall the tone of the film's narrator saying: "A peaceful landscape, an ordinary field with crows flying over it. An ordinary road, an ordinary village, vacationers, a steeple, and a fairground: this is the way to a concentration camp." I tell my father I don't understand this line but that isn't true, I understand it perfectly, I just want him to explain it in his voice, I ask if everything I saw in the film really happened or if it was made up, for example when the man says that millions of the dead haunt this land, is it true or isn't it? I beg him to tell me the truth, he replies that all of that is over now, it was a moment of madness, now it's past, don't worry, they never arrested us here, they did come into the house, they wanted to take our jewelry, we said we had nothing, they didn't ask again, you weren't born yet, they left, we were lucky. His reply does not appease me; it unnerves me all the more: you mean these murderers came right inside our house, they knocked on the door and came into our home? I lie awake all night trying to understand how these men can go on sleeping peacefully, how they can go on alive after killing thousands of people, I wonder if some of the killers were women. My father is not alone around here in wanting to gild our lives and cast a veil over what and who we are; this was a generation that brought all its children up this way, we all recall the same details: the same tastes, the same silences, the same tiny pleasures, the watermelons, the white sands at Gammarth, the lemonade, the open-air cinema, the purple olives. We all pretended not to see. And he intends a radically new life for us, he can only believe that the world must inevitably progress for the best, he rejects lingering superstitions and "passé" ideas, he wants nothing outdated in his house, he'll ensure we grow up surrounded by all that is most modern. He repeats that we must rely on kindness, morality, beauty, and justice, and that France is all of these. He says we must study, read, experience, discover, enjoy, he wants us to have a good serviceable language so we can be free everywhere and make the best of everything, not as he did. He never had any one whole language, he wasn't able to stay at school to the end. They're all slightly contorted, his Arabic, his French, his Italian, he moves between languages with ease but often confuses them and, worse, they all come out in his own odd accent. He wants us to study beautifully, that's the word he uses, because he had to go out and work at thirteen to feed his brothers and sisters, he didn't have our good fortune, that's another he likes to repeat: fortune. Your studies are your freedom, don't ever forget that.

If I'm carrying my baby father in my arms in the summer of 1909, it's in order to heft those long-past memories but also the better to hear the sounds that he used to hear and I see now that very few French words were ever at home in that house in Ariana. Mostly I recognize Arabic, with a few rare Hebrew words enfolded into it, strays from the prayer books. I pick up accents that diverge from the Tunisian dialect I know, for example, we say "ch" instead of "s," and thanks to that small nuance we can always tell who is who, I recognize a few Italian words bundled along in the torrent of Arabic and so already this house harbors a glorious intertwining of languages that speaks of his family's tortuous journey.

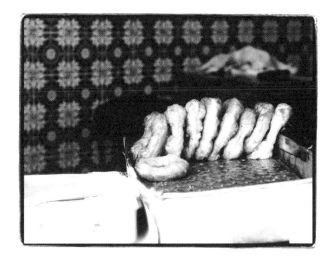

My father grew up here, without a true mother tongue, for his main language was Arabic yet he'd had to give that up to learn French at school, he then used it only to speak to his parents and, later on, his workers and clients. Hebrew made its appearance only at the important ceremonies and on Friday evenings, for the little weekly holy day. He would churn out the phrases at top speed and we liked to watch, he had just about retained the melody and meter of a lifetime of Friday evenings and that's what we found funny. He'd wear a slight, conspiratorial smile to show that we mustn't mind his mistakes, he'd be standing in front of the big dresser and we already at the table, impatient, swinging our legs, ready to giggle. He'd be clutching his tiny prayer book, we never knew if he really read from it or if he was making it all up, he would throw himself suddenly into the recitation with admirable passion and would run through it all in one go, the key thing for him being to reach the end of the service as fast as possible, so that we could answer in chorus with our two sacred syllables. He would gesture to us when our turn was coming, and we would softly chime, as if to put a full stop to his runaway prayer, the magic word, this at least unmistakable: *Amin*. Which means we concur, we believe in your words, you have spoken the truth. And he would sit down again, satisfied, he'd done his duty even while not wishing to burden us with it. Then he would unfold his napkin on his lap, hold out his glass of wine, and drink to our health. We would be wolfing the lumps of bread dipped in salt that he had set before each plate and now at last we could throw ourselves into our fine Friday evening that had the whole house smelling so good. Look now into the house of his childhood: a silver candelabra stands on the table, a glass olive oil lamp on the sideboard, with a low flame flickering within. On the patio, an old red chest decorated with birds and fish, the smell of wax, sunbeams on the mosaic floors, traces of cool water sparkling between the stone slabs. A white crocheted shawl thrown over the bed; a silk tapestry hung above it, from another time, another land. The forest and a stag to the left can be picked out, his eyes are fearful, he's just heard a noise among the leaves, he knows he's going to die, glimpsing the pack through the trees, he knows he will fall at the swamp, his strength is gone, closer inspection reveals a wound to the flank already, dripping red.

In the kitchen, mint leaves at the bottom of a glass jar, warm semolina in a great Nabeul vase, half yellow half green, spices in little earthenware pots. All is quiet. The sweet grain is flavored with cinnamon and orange-flower water. Filling the base of the vase: pomegranate juice. One of the loveliest colors in the world. In the evening, over the sacred sheen of pomegranate seeds, ancient stories revolve through the house, they multiply through retellings and gradually mutate, they say best to take care and not stand out, best to keep a low profile, not fight it out, there's always someone to point the finger even if it's not true. And so often retold: the cautionary tale of Batou, the big boss Nissim Samama's driver, that time he got into a fight and they said he'd insulted Islam. Batou Sfez was his name. One day we tell it like this: He got into a fight with the driver of a Muslim worthy, their two pony traps had run into each other and words had grown heated. One day we said he almost ran over a Muslim child, another day that the fight had been in a bar. Where each version agrees is that they emerged in their hundreds, the witnesses who hadn't been there at the time, they came to say yes, it was true, they'd seen it all, heard it all, Batou the Jew had insulted our prophet and our holy towns and our very Kaaba, he must be killed and right away. Batou repeated over and over that it wasn't true, that he had just defended himself by pushing away the man who'd attacked him, but it was too late, he was judged and condemned to death, his head was cut off before all who passed by. His story made the rounds of all our houses, all the gardens, of the stalls in the souks, the little synagogues' courtyards, it found its way into the Bey's residence, it crossed the Mediterranean, change was urgently required. That was in 1857. Among all the families, panic, terror, alarm: we are no longer safe. Then a law was passed to prevent this horror from happening again. It was what we called the Fundamental Pact: it declared that from this point onward all the Bey's subjects would have the same rights and the same duties, be they Muslim or not. That story lingered in the city walls and in children's bedrooms, we thought it was a myth, we asked to hear it again, we were frightened but we wanted to hear it, so as never to forget, so it would become part of us; this happened in our city and we were the city. Outside, through the plaster balustrades, you can see the gardens, the Café Chadly and the men playing backgammon: Kiki, Miro, Lalou, Bajou, Fraggy. The outdoor cinema. The Belhassen well. The almond and quince trees by the church. The kids playing football into the evening, who would later join Ariana's team, the Etoile Sportive. There my father was to become one of the young champions, his calves would grow strong, his body taut, he would win all the Sunday matches, defense was his game.

And then the Café des Roses, the rattle of the trams, the wheat fields laid low by the sun, the olive groves, the great farms, the bushes of Barbary figs. Farther out, the dust road leads to the oases and the desert. On the wayside, old black abandoned tires, empty crates, brushwood. French families have set up homes all around the country, to begin new lives in the sun. So many posters along the Avenue de l'Opéra spurring Parisians to leave it all behind, boasting of the climate and the easy living in this part of North Africa. The fashionable women parade up and down Avenue Jules-Ferry, they're in their element, wearing long gowns to their ankles and carrying white parasols to shade themselves from the sun, they pose for the photographer in front of the Saint-Vincent-de-Paul cathedral, they have nosegays in their hands, they don't see what they call the natives, they live on the far side of the Porte de France, behind low gates in the lanes, but also in the small mansions of the Medina and La Marsa; they see nothing of the humiliation, the submission, the injustice, the poverty, the bitterness. The so-called European city is transformed while my father grows up: at three, seven, eleven, twenty years old, he sees apartment blocks built by Italian and French architects rise and spread; as the European city gets into its stride, he joins the dance, he loves to party, loves the cinema and the comic opera and, more than anything, the Amar Brothers' great animal circus. Little by little, his life has grown wider.

At fourteen, he starts working for Monsieur Enriquez, at the end of the Avenue de Carthage. He receives clients, shows them the latest tractor models; he learns the brand names: Holt, Caterpillar, McCormick. He gives the money to his mother so she can feed the family, I'm no longer sure how many children, eight or nine, he has to work, but he is so cheerful and so polite that Monsieur Enriquez soon trusts him to run the shop, he enjoys working and never complains, that's life, that's how it is. He is disarmingly genial. His father is no longer there, he has died at fifty in his little stall in the souk, discovered dead of asphyxiation, thanks, no doubt, to a blowtorch. He used to make silverware and jewelry: necklaces and bracelets, candlesticks and the votive *candils* to hang among the tombs. All day he'd be bent over his silverware, soldering, shaping, starting again, people said he was a saint. His name was Hai, which means *life* in Hebrew, he who lives. He was my grandfather and he quietly passed the taste of his name down to me, the taste of life before death, sacred life.

At fourteen, my father obtains his school certificate and so leaves school, his head already full of the operetta arias and lines from Racine that he would lovingly safeguard. More than a stock of treasures, these come to represent what he hopes to nurture among his children: the best language, high culture, that which will save them from everything. What he has been unable to pursue, his children will pursue; he will do everything to furnish the resources. On Fridays after two glasses of wine, after dinner, it was never religious songs that filled our house but, to accompany the toasted pistachios and honey-soaked pastries, he would sing "La Belle de Cadix" with her velvet eyes who calls for your love, and we'd sing the chorus all together chica chica chic! Ay ay ay! Or, most often, he'd call for silence and, laughing but proud, launch into the opening scene of *Esther*. Every time we would applaud and demand an encore, giggling at his prettily rolled *r*'s: Morrre, *Papa*, rrrecite Rrracine for us, *Papa*! He was never riled by our teasing: the children could do no wrong and, in any case, both in the family and in the rest of his life, he had taken a stance of inferiority and nobody could have shifted him out of it. Now, children, as you know this is only the opening, Act I, scene 1. I don't know any of it after that. "Is that you, dear Elise? Oh thrice happy day! Blessed be the heavens that send you to my prayers, You who, like me a child of Benjamin and once my childhood's constant companion. And who, suffering the weight of our same yoke, Helped me to bear the misfortunes of Zion." That was his own prayer. And my mother, of course, would be rolling her eyes again.

When Monsieur Enriquez dies, my father buys his own shop, ten meters away on the same side of the Avenue de Carthage, at number 79, and he puts a great yellow sign over the door: Henry Fellous, Machines Agricoles. He buys it with my mother's dowry. He's twenty-nine, my mother's brothers trust him: Bice will be happy with him, he's a good man, he'll be able to buy his shop and give our sister a diamond engagement ring, they will surely be happy together. The brothers will share their father's legacy of property holdings between them, but as a girl, my mother stands to inherit nothing, just the dowry. In the wedding photo my father looks like Jacques-Emile Blanche's portrait of Proust. I set the two photos side by side on a shelf in my library; I've been looking at them for years without truly paying them any attention, they are the guardians of my library.

Behind the photo, books by Nietzche, Musil, Goethe. My mother smiles, her dress is magnificent, my father holds the net veil lightly, she will describe how she tried to make this day the loveliest of her life but didn't quite manage, her brothers said: You'll see, love will come gradually, don't worry, Henry will be a good husband and a good father. My parents move into the building that has just been completed on the Avenue de Paris, right beside the big synagogue; it's here that their five children, four boys and one girl, will be born. It's here that they will pass on to us their reverence for school and books, their taste for cinema, music, and dancing. As for them, after a few years not of grand passion but of mutual goodwill, they are reduced to arguing over nothing, we never see them kiss, my mother reproaches Henry for having dirty hands from the machines, and he accepts it all without riposte, he goes on saying he loves her, though without much conviction. Occasionally on the eves of holy days, he teases her, singing *L'Auberge du cheval blanc* in a gently suggestive voice and this drives my mother wild, she rolls her eyes and enlists us as her witnesses: he is so coarse! Laughing, he edges a little closer to her, and, laying his cheek upon hers, sings: "One day to be loved by you, I would give my life for you, yours is the spell upon me, oh take pity on me, kiss away my cares and say you love me too."

My mother loses patience, he sings that song to her every time they argue, and she tells him again, he truly is vulgar and, really, to sing like that in front of the children, it's quite unforgivable. We always laugh though we don't understand, we never want to take sides, we don't see what's so vulgar about it, we would also like her to say it to him, that she loves him too, and why not? The years go by, the children grow up as best they can, school provides them with a voluptuous stability: home offers a mixture of affection and tension, at school the whole world is waiting to be discovered. They grow hungry for more, they are insatiable, they leave for France as soon as they graduate, they're not at all afraid of facing another country alone, they don't come back to Tunisia. Except for me. I don't know why I come back every year, several times a year, with such passion.

I think that I come back to see, to reassess, in order more easily to disengage. Anyway, that's what I've been telling myself, so far. I pretend that this country has become my literary material, that it's not my own story that I'm describing, that I don't come back to try to recover the past; no, rather it's in order not to lose the very fabric of the city, to move forward with its story, to understand how we have gotten here, how tourists can have been murdered on the beach and in the Bardo museum by young Tunisians. To try, too, to see how our own lives have been entirely created by political history despite our thinking that they were ours alone, that they were "personal." I return to the mysterious, ever-delicate voice of Borges, from when he went blind. "I know the things I've lost are so many that I could not begin to count them and that those losses now, are all I have. I know that I've lost the yellow and the black and I think of those unreachable colors as those that are not blind cannot."

My father takes my hand, it's Sunday, we walk to Belvedere Park, we feed crusts of bread to the swans, I'm about twelve. We buy toffee apples and barley sugar, a quick turn on the merry-go-round, and already it's the end of the day, he points to the sky and says that everyone in the world sees the same sky, look how beautiful it is, look how big it is, we're all the same for we all see the same sky. He doesn't know yet that, like so many others, he'll have to leave this, his country, at sixty, that it can no longer be his future, he'll have to build a new life for himself in France, he'll have to leave everything here, to leave with nothing. And in leaving, he will moreover leave behind so many gestures, smells, tastes, so much knowledge that his forebears also left to this city, in their turn. No, he doesn't know this yet, his face is radiant, he's showing me the sky, he has so much confidence in life that I'm astonished, I look now at his eyes looking up at the sky and I think my father is so good, perhaps too good, even, he will be hurt, he's so fragile, so helpless, all this I feel confusedly as I walk with him beneath the Belvedere's great palms and I squeeze his hand a little tighter, I never want to let go of this hand. And so, to lull myself to sleep in my little bed under the window, I lie looking for hours at the vast sky and all the stars scattered over it like the Mikado sticks on the Kairouan carpet, and I speak to it, I humbly ask the sky to protect this family of mine, this truly haphazard and defenseless family, and suddenly it's as though I'm speaking to other children great distances away, hidden in the stars or perhaps themselves huddled in their beds, and I repeat very softly: Yes, it's true what my father said in the park, we all see the same thing, we are all the same, good night. At the foot of my bed, Catia, my little cat, shifts around a bit and settles again more comfortably on my feet, I gaze at the white wall above my pillow, it has grown like the screen of an enormous cinema, I wrap myself in sleep.

This is what my father told me one summer in Cannes, at the Café de la Plage. It was nine in the morning. He was wearing a red polo shirt, he still had sunglasses on but I could see his eyes well enough. Our hands were clasped, one over the other, beside our coffee cups, it was the first time we'd been alone like this, in France, in the middle of August. We had ordered *pains aux raisins*, he called them *schneiks*, you might have taken us for lovers but no, he was my father. I was twenty-seven. Now he could talk to me because I was a woman and could understand life. Before, you were my little wild child, I couldn't explain things to you, but now it's the right time, I might die soon and I wouldn't want you to mistake me for some other man. I squeezed his hand a little harder to let him know that he needn't say these things, he would always be my father and I loved him as he was. He squeezed mine lightly in answer, he'd understood. Then he began to speak. I never deceived you children. I loved my wife, loved her so, so deeply, I still admire her because she knows so many things, she's an artist, she's very cultivated, but she has a condition, she has never loved love. I explained it to the boys at the start of the summer, I wanted you all to know the real truth. They're men, they understood, they said you're right, *Papa*, we don't blame you, you couldn't do anything else. She never liked it, she said it horrified her, she thought my hands were dirty, she didn't want me to touch her, we would argue over nothing, she kept on saying that she liked cleanliness and that I didn't really know what that meant. I'm going to tell you something and you mustn't be shocked: I've always liked women, that's how I've been since I was fifteen, I can't go without, I love life, I love to celebrate, I love to laugh. I was unlucky with *Maman*, I thought it would get better with time but it got worse. And then she fell ill. I tried everything to help her and heal her, but she always relapsed, she said she had anxiety, there was no solution, even the doctors tried but they failed, always the anxiety, always in bed. When you were born, she wasn't sick yet, it's when you all started to leave that she fell ill. When you were born, I remember she told me: I don't want any more lovemaking with you now, it's enough, I have a daughter, that's what I wanted, and now that's over. So I took her at her word, I didn't touch her again, but I was forced to find another way, that's all, I didn't deceive you. Only I couldn't tell you before, you see. But everybody in Tunis knew. Except for you children, and except for *Maman*, of course. Everybody said: Poor Henry, his wife neglects him, it's natural he should go elsewhere, you can't blame him, you can understand, but he loves his family so much, he's a good father, such a sad story.

I ordered another coffee. So did he. We stayed about an hour more, people started setting up on the beach, opening their sun umbrellas, getting into their swimsuits, laying out their towels, looking at the sea, the light was hazy and so delicate still; I talked to him about my life, I told him he'd done his best and that he'd looked after us all very well, I thanked him, he'd been a good father and we were lucky to be here, the two of us, in this café, able to speak openly, it's the loveliest time for the beach when you come very early in the morning, don't you think? I spoke to him of our childhood beaches, of Gammarth, of the Hôtel de France at Hammamet, of the years when there were only two hotels in that little town and we used to eat white bread with chocolate after bathing, when we were all wrapped in our towels and shivering, did he remember? Yes, it was lovely, he said. Not a word more. I tried to talk too of how he left Tunisia. Was he still thinking about his shop, hadn't he found it difficult to drop everything and leave with nothing? To leave at sixty and start all over again here? He didn't reply. He said only it's fine, it's fine. Now I'm going to the market, like in Tunis, and I'll go to the beach, just for an hour or so, to cool down. After that I'll head home for my nap. It was good for us to meet, my wild one, he hoped I'd understood what he'd told me.

The waiter came to take our cups, he wanted to set the tables for lunch, my father said of course, thank you, we're just going, we won't trouble you any longer.

I took his hand once more, I reassured him, yes, I understood, I didn't blame him. But I also spoke up for my mother. I reminded him that she'd suffered so much in life and that now she was alone, while he… He said yes, that's true, you're right, but there you go, that's life, we weren't right for each other, that's all, luckily we had you. You were our blessing and for you, only for you, we loved each other nonetheless, as best we could.

We stood, together we looked out at the beach and the sea, trying silently to hold on to the morning's beauty, then he crossed the road, it was an important day for us both. I watched him walk away down the Croisette boulevard. He turned, squinting his eyes and waving to me, so I smiled and returned the gesture, raising my hand and squinting back, yes, I loved him too.

"Una furtiva lagrima" glides from the computer onto the table, Pavarotti's voice envelops the whole room, settling on fabrics, paintings, plants, carpets, and fruit, *Ah cielo, si può morir*, it names them one by one, exalts them, and, along with the voice, I invite forgotten years, gardens, people to enter the house once more. The voice repeats *Ah cielo, si può morir d'amor*. I look at each object for the last time, following the lead of that majestic invisible voice. The terracotta vase that Mathilde gave me stands on the bookcase from Kathmandu, next to Guy de Maupassant (*Notre Coeur, or A Woman's Pastime*), Stefan Zweig (*Erasmus of Rotterdam*), and Jean-Bertrand Pontalis (*Love of Beginnings*); it is in good company.

Look, I found this while tidying the cupboards, it's from before Christ, I can't say the exact date but I know you like pots and I'm clearing out the house, I need to get rid of everything. There's something hidden inside, can you hear it moving around in there? It can't be gotten out, or only if you really want to know what it is, you'd have to break the vase and then you'd have nothing but the pieces, it would be a shame.

When Mathilde laughs, you can see the gap in her front teeth.

True, I can hear something like a heart turning over in there, thank you so much, I'll keep it safe, I'd rather not know what's inside, only listen to it like this, it must have come from the far depths of the sea or perhaps it was even made from the earth of Carthage?

Mathilde lives in Carthage, close to the Baths of Antoninus, her villa looks over the sea, her gardener was fifteen when he started working for her and now he's about to become a grandfather. She comes to see me regularly, she brings almond cookies, roses, or stems of bougainvillea from her garden, she talks about Renan, Chateaubriand, Gide, about her Normandy life, she says we must give Tunisia time to regain its balance, but she is confident, it will be okay, it will work out. We never spend long together but she gives key moments, even the most intimate experiences of her life to me, such as the young priest she met on a Paris–Bordeaux train when she was seventeen. It was a very hot day, she had a fan and he laid his black notebook on his knees, they talked a little, mostly they looked at each other, he had sought to see her again for months afterward, he wrote her ardent letters, but she had not dared to undermine his path as a cleric. Yet he had beautiful eyes, perhaps I made a terrible mistake. Something like Habib Bourguiba's eyes, she adds. Just to give you an idea, but he wrote with such style, yes, he had style, I've kept all his letters, I'll show them to you when I next think of it. His name was Louis. She laughs again. I love her laugh which punctuates her words and sets them off kilter, just where it's least expected. Serious, then suddenly arch, even childish. One day I said to her thank you, Mathilde, she said I hate it when people call me Mathilde, so now I make a special effort, I call her either Madame Riadh or Madame Carpentier, I never know which she'd prefer but I believe she finds both acceptable. She came to Tunisia as a young girl, with a golden-blonde ponytail and red pumps, she even remembers her royal-blue dress very narrow at the waist with white stitching at the neckline, when she disembarked at La Goulette, a very pretty dress. She had been offered work as a secretary, she'd accepted, she had made the journey but she'd never imagined that Tunisia would become her country. A few years later she had married the businessman from Sousse who was her boss, Monsieur Riadh; she always addressed him as Monsieur although he mostly called her Mathilde, except when they made love, then it was Monsieur and Madame, excuse me if I'm saying too much, but it's to give you an idea of the gentleman.

Were you in love?

She doesn't know how to describe her love for him, she hunts for the right word while staring at the blue glass lamp on the patio, no, she can't put her finger on it, it's hard to say: in love—perhaps not, but she can say that she loved him, yes, she loved him very much. Oh, I've found the way to say it: in love, no, but loving, yes, without a doubt. Respectful most of all, affectionate, admiring. And then there's Nora, of course, our child, our darling.

Here's an example to explain our connection for you. When he had his coffee, he used to do like this, he'd put a spoonful of sugar in, then he'd hand the cup to me to stir it with the teaspoon, we'd both hear the sound of the spoon against the cup and we thought it was a great thing that held us together; it's a little silly but that's how it was. He could never drink his coffee without doing that, and actually that's what I miss most, that moment when I'd stir his coffee for him.

Mathilde laughs again. Yes, that little sound of the spoon against the cup, his waiting, what united us just then, it's strange don't you think, so strange that all that remains are these little details, although we had a whole life together?

Later I learned how their story ended. They had separated, abruptly, fifteen years ago; she had just turned fifty-five, he was ten years older. She described the scene to me several times. I'll never forget it, she adds. One day, in their blue room, it was time for coffee, he had just returned from Mecca, he said to her, you're rather old, little wife, I want to divorce you and marry the fifteen-year-old I have met in Dubai, I love her and she loves me. Mathilde replied: What are you saying? She left the room, she walked once around the garden, looked up at the tall cypresses and the swallows; from now on all that she loved would be reduced to the colors and the sounds of this land. Then she went back inside, her head was spinning: I think you said something to me just now, can you repeat it, please? And her husband repeated: You are old, little wife, I want a divorce, I'm going to marry a fifteen-year-old who I met three weeks ago, I love her and she loves me.

Mathilde says he bought her, that girl, she has proof, she can't reveal more to me but she knows. She also knows that he was under a spell, such things happen in this country, you can't pretend they don't happen, even if you don't believe, you have to allow for them. There are witches, wicked people, poisonings, curses. But now she doesn't even blame the husband anymore, besides he sends her all kinds of tokens of respect, his bitter orange preserves, whole pistachios from his estate. And then, life has flown by, her grandchildren are soon to pass their baccalaureate exams, they're twins, a boy and a girl, lovely children; she often takes them on vacation to Normandy, she was born at the heart of the country in the *bocage* region, close to Villers, the twins love those parts too, especially in cherry season, there's a giant cherry tree, as tall as this, the amount of fruit it produces, we make *clafoutis*, jams, tarts, we're eating them right to the very end of the summer and they're delicious. Well, have a lovely evening, see you again next Tuesday. I'll come by, keep the Renan, take your time. She always lowers her voice to say goodbye, as if at the end of a song.

She disappears down the staircase, and now my evening can begin.

I pour myself a glass of muscat from Kélibia, looking out to sea, I let the night flow into the house, and the stories return, little by little, they return to life, they rediscover their voices, everything becomes magnetic, everything gathers into an invisible pattern. So many women who've confided their life stories to me and, with very few exceptions, the elements are always the same. I think of Madame Henry, of Isis, Juliette, Faouzia, of my mother. In each woman, this admixture of helplessness, great freedom, and fantasy. Women living alone, who've been abandoned or who have chosen their solitude. Capable of anything upon a whim, perhaps even of dying, leaping from a window, like Kriss, gorgeous Kriss who, one summer night in Marseille had just said good night to her lover with a sweet, sweet smile, had kissed him on the cheek as if going to bed and then, right in front of him, where he stood, she had slowly walked out onto the balcony and thrown herself off.

Of them all, Madame Henry is the most fanciful. With a single sip of Kélibia muscat, she reappears, every hair intact. Her face, her gait and bearing, her dramatic gestures, so I would really understand. The rise and fall of her voice, she too like a song. She lives in a thatched house at the Ry turnoff, on the road to Buchy. I like that her surname is my father's first name. At the age of forty, she left her husband, when her father-in-law died. In her distress, she'd realized that it wasn't her husband she had loved but his father, a superb man, cultivated and amusing, who used to live with them, a well-built man, she says: she draws his body in the air, so I can picture him. When that gentleman died, she had looked again at her husband and found suddenly that there was no substance to him, suddenly it was plain that he'd always been colorless, dull, coarse, and clumping. How had she managed, never a real conversation, not one fine gesture. She'd always seen the father in the shape of the son: she is trying to explain it to me and at the same time she is wondering if a love like that is possible. So this is what she did: she took her son and daughter and she moved them all to Ry. Luckily they were already quite grown-up, that made it simpler. She never saw her Gustave again, she thinks he must be dead now. She recalls the moment she decided to leave him. She was in the kitchen peeling some carrots and all at once, she did a funny thing, she slipped the knife blade under her wedding ring. She frightened herself, so she went to lie down on the bed, she lay and thought, thought deeply, and then after half an hour she got up and said that's it, I'm leaving him. Up to that point, they'd been living near Gisors, in the La Lévrière valley, in a huge house, all windows, with views over the river, they wanted for nothing, life was easy, the neighbors envied them and tried to be like them. She had set up her own small business selling built-in kitchens and that had allowed her to live comfortably for several years, she'd even been able to put some money aside.

She had moved to Ry to be closer to the landscape of her childhood. Her parents used to have a farm near there. It had been difficult during the war. She would smile very strangely every time she mentioned that farm, her gaze would look back to skies invisible to me, but she never said more, and I never asked her any questions. If you only knew, I could have made a novel out of my life, but it's too late now. Only if you… I would be happy to tell you a chapter every day and you could do what you liked with it, I present you with my life, here it is. She had told me this all in one go, on our first day, when she came to meet me at the station in the white Mercedes. It was José who had sent her instead of himself, the two foals had been born, he couldn't leave them, especially as one had had a difficult birth.

She laughed, tossing her head back fiercely. She used to wear a trench coat like Humphrey Bogart, black patent loafers, tortoiseshell glasses, and a fine designer scarf, yellow and black with Moroccan stallions on it, lean and spirited. A real movie star. We drove the length of the forest, she was straight-backed, she held the wheel with great finesse and seemed all considered like a character in a novel. From time to time, she would turn to me and smile to check she still had my attention, she was sure that in her I had at last found the subject of one of my next books, I would respond with a polite smile and she'd go on with her story.

I loved that part of Normandy, the beech woods, the wild hedgerows, the roads with their regular turnings onto fields of rape or fallow meadows, the chickadees coming and going all day long between the telephone wires and the mailboxes where their chicks were growing; I opened the window, I wanted to catch the smell of the forest. At one point: I'm in love, I have to tell you. Then she told me about Julien, the evenings when he would come to see her and they'd hide in the garden, behind the big lime tree, she had never felt such physical pleasure as with this young man of thirty-two. I know what I'm saying is a bit shocking as I'll be sixty in two months but he's incredible and I think he's never felt like this before either, at least that's what he implies, with all his unexpected demands but my goodness they're not unwelcome, and besides, actions don't lie, do they? Occasionally, in sudden contrast with her outward appearance, she would adopt a salacious tone that I found embarrassing, still I looked down as I smiled so as not to hurt her, pretending to smooth my skirt over my knees. She didn't want her grandchildren to know anything of this adventure, they thought Julien was just a neighbor with time on his hands, who visited to gossip with their grandmother, so she preferred to meet him in secret and never in the house. They would go into the woods, into the sunken pathways, once even behind the Beauvoir church, the view across the Pays de Bray valley had been exhilarating, but no one had seen a thing that day, mmm, yes, Julien is quite insatiable and I'm the same: it's a wonderful chapter that we're enjoying together, you know.

Do your grandchildren live with you?

Yes, she's looked after the three little ones, Léon, Maxime, and Justine, since they were born. Léon is sixteen and a half now and he's also in love, so it goes on, it's a blessing. Three children her daughter had with three different men. She's unstable, my daughter, but that's another story. Commonplace men, all three. She gets pregnant with the first boy in her bed and, after a month, she gives the baby to me, here, *Maman*, I don't have time: that's Jeanne, that's how she is. For now, they're very sweet but I don't know how I'm going to manage bringing them up and finding professions for them, besides Justine is deaf-mute but you know that doesn't stop her from keeping secrets, I found letters she's been writing from her boarding school to a girl called Germaine, that's also another story, she's still only fifteen but I can tell you we're in for quite a ride with that one.

Madame Henry explains that her theatrical gestures come from a habit she's gotten into with Justine, being wordless and obliged to speak with their bodies. If we happen to meet again, I'll introduce you to Julien, but please, don't show you know about us, it would upset him, I can count on you, can't I? The car smelled of Madame Henry, a mixture of hairspray and slightly oversweet perfume, almost gilded: with each visit she made, this scent came with her, for me it became the perfume of her voice.

And in this house in Tunisia, having brought her back with the golden glow of a sip of muscat, I realize suddenly that I've gone from green to blue, I've replaced Madame Henry with Mathilde, and Normandy has receded away beyond the Mediterranean, its forests beyond my window of blue. Forests and Normandy both so distant but still at the center of my life. The two countries are superimposed one over the other, they reinforce, magnetize, and illuminate each other, they are inscribed in my body. My first encounter with Madame Henry was about twenty years ago. At the time I liked to gather stories from that corner of the world that I'd adopted, but I can't remember them all, I should have taken notes. I was enlightened, regaled, lied to, I was always there, ready to meet their words, I never wearied of it. I also used to like running behind the combine harvesters when we were meant to help make the bales, I used to laugh because here were my father's farm machines in actual wheat fields, I recognized their great red, green, or yellow steel bodies and the huge ridged tires that went writing across the earth.

These machines were my antique writing, practically forgotten, only reappearing now in landscapes that I'd discovered late and that had, nonetheless, shaped me, teaching me this taste for language and for France. I was not to set foot in France until I reached seventeen. The apple trees, the wheat fields, the vines, the harvests, the seasons all cycled through my first grammar and comprehension books. Normandy was their main character, she skipped in between the words and syllables, between the dictations and the verb tables, I wanted to go there, I wanted to live in the book, to jump feet-first right into the paper and find myself there,

in the land of my dreams, on the far side of the sea, in the
midst of an orchard in flower, what delight that would be,
free at last. In Tunisia I was in exile, something rang false,
I couldn't put my finger on it, yet it genuinely was my native country and I seemed to be a happy child. I learned
young to be torn in two, not to be shocked by the feeling, to
breathe through it. To love leaving and then returning, to be
always between two or three cities, to keep several languages
equally in play and even not to understand everything of a
place in order better to grasp the sensations, the nuances.

When I arrived at that house on the edge of the forest
of Lyons, I was as keen to listen to the sounds of the countryside as to the locals' confessions. One time I brought a
Japanese nightingale with me from Paris, the vendor having
assured me that he was a virtuosic singer; he had even used
the word "exceptional." I made my journey by train, the cage
on my lap, I wanted to show the nightingale my new ter-
ritory, I was impatient to see his reaction. I'd had him for
three days but no sound had yet emerged from his yellow
bill. I thought that in the countryside he would rediscover
his song. Throughout the journey, he fluttered inside his
cage, watching me anxiously; from time to time I raised the
cage up to the window so he could see the landscape but still
not one note. I was disappointed but I admired the colors of
his little body: some blue, some yellow, some almost-red, he
was magnificent, I whispered to him, I shall call you Bazou.
When we arrived, it was evening and I set the cage down
in the living room. Still nothing. In the morning, when I
opened the window that looks over the orchard, the first
murmurings of chickadees and blackbirds floated into the
house, he leaned toward the sounds and launched into an

extraordinary sequence, as if he were a conductor whose entire orchestra of instruments were contained in his voice.
The countryside responded and his song grew more com-
plex with each variation, and carried with it all the birds in
the garden. With and through my nightingale, I began to
listen with close attention to the movements of birds in the
hedges, on chimney pots or telephone wires or even a little
farther out, birds coming from the forest, from beyond the
beeches, harder to distinguish yet so precise, what a joy it
was to take in all these miniature languages. I watched for
the leaves' rustling, different each time depending on the
tree, whether in the garden or the forest or my memory.
The sounds became faces, I exalted them, I perceived their
nuances, I registered their delicacy, I compared them, I recalled them, I wouldn't miss a single one, each had its place
in the randomness of things, it was a magnificent orches-
tration. Little by little, the songs turned into stories. Where
Joseph lives now Mère Richard used to have her café, she
frightened everyone up and down the forest but she offered
a warm welcome to the woodcutters and the workers from
the glass factory, there was always good cheer in her cottage.
But the factory has gone, the workers too, the hamlet has
emptied out. After she closed her café, we used to see old
Mère Richard tramping kilometers across the fields to do
odd mending and darning jobs among the wealthy, and it
was painful to see her returning the same way at night. Bit
by bit she wore herself out, she died alone in the forest, we
used to hear the crows sobbing in her voice. In the end she
became really frightening, with her filthy hair and everything, she stank like an animal. It's wild around here, you
know, Paris isn't far but it's stayed the same here for the

last two hundred years. There's our tall Lucie who at sixteen gave birth to her kid, as she calls him, all by herself in the upstairs bedroom, without a word to her parents who were sitting down in the kitchen, with their hot chocolate and knitting by the fire. It was nine in the evening, things started to move, she hadn't even told them she was pregnant, with her wide skirts no one had noticed, we hadn't even had time to really look at each other, we didn't even have mirrors, anyway she cut the cord with her teeth and cleaned herself up with the heavy towels, she was used to it from the calving, she didn't have much trouble getting the hang of it. She took some deep breaths and went downstairs still shaky, the little one in her arms, wrapped hastily in the bedclothes, she could hardly stand up but she had to show her parents. They said nothing only asked why she was so pale and what she was hiding in her sweater. She said: It's my kid, I cut the cord myself, I think he's okay. They went on like it was nothing, got on with bringing him up no questions asked, we're not big talkers around here. They taught me not to be shocked at anything. Looks as though you've not seen much action, why the face, a baby is nothing, it's like a calf, nothing to be afraid of.

And the father?

He was a truck driver, the man you call the father. He'd spent a month living at the farm and helping the family, he was from Forges, and that's what I got up to at sixteen, he won't even know I had a baby, I never saw him again. Now it's strange my kid drives big buses, though I never told him, he goes around the schools taking the little ones home, but I don't see much of him these days, I don't like his new girl-friend, she's a troublemaker.

Tall Lucie told me her secret in the kitchen, calmly, while I helped her to tie a rabbit à la moutarde. This time too I had to keep it to myself, for even her husband didn't know. I knew how to keep secrets, I protected them, they were so fragile, I promised her I'd say nothing to José. Also that day she had given me news of little Virginie who had been adopted by the chimney sweep, you remember how you loved her when she was only two and was always jumping up for cuddles, you wouldn't recognize her now, she must weigh about a hundred kilos, she's filthy and she won't work, she says she has a lump under her breast and it must be a disease, I think it's probably a lump of dirt, she'll say anything so she can do nothing, poor François doesn't know what more to say, she can turn nasty, he's frightened of her, skinny thing that he is. I should say he thought he'd saved her from her alcoholic parents but nothing of the sort, she was a charming little thing it's true but you remember her expression like a smacked puppy, she turned out badly, you see, she'll be twenty soon and ugly as anything, it's tough luck for François, he frets over her and what's more, with all she eats, she's not cheap.

Here, they told me stories amid laughter, always rather loopy tales that led one into the next so as to make me dizzy, of course they'd exaggerate to impress me, they aimed both to frighten and to make me laugh. This always went on during the Sunday feasts in local farms' courtyards, we'd drink cider, roast a boar or suckling pig on the spit, we made mirabelle tarts, sometimes there were carnival games or sack races, José would make sangria (his specialty), which was always well received, it was his family's recipe: it's a taste you just can't get here, impossible to find, it comes from

Andalusia! This is what he'd say with each glass he served to the cluster of guests settled under the cherry tree: the cheese maker, the joiner, the electrician, the carpenter, the blacksmith, the mail carrier, all were represented there with their families; when it came to a party they were punctual, they dressed up for the occasion in bright colors and flower-print blouses, their chignons done by the hairdresser we called Madame Sahara, I never knew why. I listened to them and at the same time I would gaze down the line of beeches that ran along the road, the trunks battered by storms, the deep-blue skies beyond the fields, and the crows skimming over the earth, I was inside a picture book.

Monsieur Frank, let's talk about Monsieur Frank, now that we've let our hair down a bit—put in Fernand Delalande, who lived on the other side of the trailers, right behind the baron's house, he'd been a sports journalist in Rouen but he didn't go out so much now. José, you used to know Monsieur Frank quite well, so tell us the story, for a laugh, that man's a mystery to me, I don't get all the comings and goings on the road all day long.

But everyone's known about him for ages now apart from you, Fernand, only no one said a word because they were still a bit nervous and he was quite a big guy, no one wanted to mess with him. Here's the truth for you now, if you really want to know: Monsieur Frank had a slave in his garden, yes, you heard me right and not a hint of a lie: a slave. The boy was thirteen when he started working for him and he died at fifty-five in the stable, where he slept his whole life. But this is shameful, Fernand said over and over while José was telling the story, it's shameful that we let this happen in our own times, you should have called social services on him, how is this possible? José waved his hand in the air to say steady on, he hadn't finished the story. Now and then, when he closed his eyes or shrugged to show his goodwill and say life is like that, you have to accept things, he reminded me of my father. With showman-like long pauses, he went on with his story. In the end, the boy grew old (though Monsieur Frank always called him *the boy*), he was riddled with disease, his teeth were rotten, he had boils everywhere that got infected, big as your thumb, all red, yellow, brown, black, dreadful. One Tuesday, the vet had warned Monsieur Frank, he threatened him with fists raised: If you don't call a doctor, I'll denounce you to the police. But it was too late, by the Thursday morning, the boy was gone, dead as a doornail. He was found in with the animals. It was a heart attack, but on the back of an appalling infection. He was worn out, naturally. It seems he had the arteries of a hundred-year-old. And to pass the time, that thug Monsieur Frank would go thieving all day in his cattle van, like that, up and down past all our houses, but not because he was bored or looking for someone, no, no, no, you mustn't believe that. He was spotting local animals, then he'd go stealing our sheep and chickens while everyone was asleep. At first we all thought it was a fox but the fox was him, I have evidence but I can't share it. Now he's gotten his comeuppance, he's a total invalid and his wife has to keep the house going, the Parakeet we call her. Such a nice old lady, so honest, it's incomprehensible how people around here get together. José is contorted with laughter as he tells the story. And the mayor's wife, you know that one, at least? No, what's wrong with the mayor's wife? I knew it, you Parisians don't know you're born, we have to teach you everything.

Don't tell them everything, sweetheart, it'll backfire on us, warns tall Lucie, pouring him a sixth glass of cider. No, but they have to know a bit of what goes on around here, they can't stay in their bubble forever. So here you go. When she was a bit younger, that Chantal, and perhaps even a bit these days, she used to set up in that kind of trailer on the forest road, behind the path to the swamp, and she took all comers. All our men showed up there at some point, they don't say it but we're up to speed. Are you sure? The mayor's wife? That can't be right. You'll have to ask her what's right! As for him, you think he's a saint but he's got at least three court cases on his back, which is already crooked as they come.

José and tall Lucie were my principal informers; giving a voice to their little corner of the world made them happy. When I was with them, I forgot everything else, I was drawn into their baroque tales, I found I wanted to learn about life on the farms, about field enclosure, about what went on here during the war, about their grandad's black-market dealings. Madame Henry told me she'd said nothing to them about her love for Julien because they were gossips, at which they laughed fit to burst; they explained that the Julien in question used to go about making eyes at all the girls around here, young and old, and he was a dreadful thief too, of another kind, he'd even swindled them at the Gournay races, and what do you think he was up to with Madame Henry, he only took all her savings, that's what, he thinks he's invincible with his angelic curls and periwinkle eyes, she thought she'd found herself a gallant knight, well I can assure you she copped a real handsome crook. And keeping her Jojo living there in a trailer at the bottom of the garden, d'you think that's all right? He's her handyman, I don't know if he even pays her anything for the place, he's a bit simple but still. As for her, poor thing, she has such a rose-tinted view of the world, she falls for everything, you know what that means, *rose-tinted*? José, who spoke a rich mixture of French and Normandy dialect spiced with Picardy terms and rounded off with his Spanish accent, always took the Parisians, as he called us, for ignoramuses who knew nothing about anything and so he'd explain. He explained everything: what we should eat, how to light a fire or nurse a flu, how the president and his ministers would do better listening to him than following up the idiocies they commit year in, year out, he always had a plan to make everything work—if only the bigwigs knew he existed, they would come right to the hamlet to consult him and follow his advice, that was clear. But I don't say a word, he would say again. I don't say a word, I never do. And at this he would close his eyes to show his superiority, and his sense of mischief. That was José and we loved him, warts and all.

But the love affair between Julien and Madame Henry did not last more than a year, he had indeed hoodwinked her with his enchanting eyes: he'd acquired a stable of horses at a huge farm on the Lyons road out of the money she'd saved up over the years and that she had given him out of love, she insisted you have to give young people a good start. It all really went to pieces the afternoon Léon went to look for Julien, to bring him a bowl of raspberries from his grandmother, and found him with his Clémentine happily in his lap. Clémentine was sixteen and had golden hair. Léon could not stand by and watch his grandmother's boyfriend with their lovely innocent Clémentine in his arms; that very evening he decided to sign up for the Foreign Legion. This time it was Léon who came to tell me what had happened, the following morning. He was disgusted with life: I know you'll understand but please don't tell my grandmother, I'm going, there's nothing more for me here, I'm going as far away as possible, she doesn't know yet, it's this or die. Léon used to do odd jobs for me now and then, he'd put up shelves, mow the lawn, stack the firewood, repair the lights. I don't know what became of him.

And little by little I also lost track of Madame Henry, they said she had retreated, that she lost faith in everything after leaving Julien, she didn't even want to go back to our part of the world, too full of painful memories. I didn't even catch her at the Saturday market in Ry. Twenty years washed over that little Haute-Normandie community—until, last year, I spot a white car stopping before my gate and Madame Henry steps swiftly into the garden: Do you recognize me? She was wearing a pretty lavender-blue linen dress with a round white-trimmed collar, a golden light came through the forest behind her.

Of course I recognize you, Louise. It's been such a long time.

I'd like to speak to you. There's something I'd like to ask of you.

Then beneath the pergola, over a spiced tea, she told me. She asked if I would now agree to write a book about her life; you remember I already had this idea?

Yes, of course, I remember. But you know books really don't work like that. Forgive me, I love listening to you but no, I couldn't do that.

Listen to me, then, and you can think about it afterward, you don't have to give me your answer today, take your time. You should know that I haven't told a soul what I'm about to tell you. Her voice was soft and slow. I did tell you that I lived on a farm close to Ry during the war, didn't I—do you remember?

Yes indeed, I remember.

In fact, my parents lost all their property at that point and a farmer moved into our farm, we became his employees and I, at thirteen, I had to labor for him, I carried the milk pails, it was heavy work, I looked after the animals, I rose at five every morning, I did the mucking out before going to school, but I had no choice, my parents couldn't say a word, the farmer used to watch me like a lecher as he smoked his smuggled cigarettes, he used to smile at me, he was hideous, he had no front teeth, I was frightened of him. One morning, the great swine took me into a stable and had his way with me. I wept, I struggled but my parents were still asleep, they couldn't hear me, and he had put a handkerchief over my mouth, he laughed as he pulled his trousers up. Of course I was pregnant. I was sent to Rouen to an establishment that looked after girls in my condition, I was asked if I wanted to leave the baby with them when I gave birth, I said yes, they asked me to sign, I signed my name, Louise Henry. The baby was born, I left it there and I didn't say a word to anyone, only my parents knew, it was our secret; I was relieved, I wanted to start my life afresh, at last I could be free, after my incarceration. At eighteen, I met my husband, I told you how much I loved his father and that whole little situation. I agreed to marry him on condition that we all live together. We had a girl and a boy and life went on one way

or another. What with my daughter's not being well and all
the troubles that brought, and having to look after her three
children for her, I've had a hard life, it's true, but with some
happy moments all the same. Best of all was Julien who lit
up my life, but that's another story, I've put it behind me
now, I don't even blame him, he was so young, and anyway,
I don't like the word *blame*, most of it's lame, you know.
Anyway, here's what I came to tell you. Last month I was
at home in the middle of making my famous raspberry jam,
I've brought you a jar, by the way, it's delicious and I know
you like jam, so someone rings my doorbell and there I see
a frightful old spinster of about sixty, quite unwashed, who
says in a raspy old voice: "Why did you abandon me, tell me
why?" Yes: it was my daughter. She said she'd been looking and at last had found me. And she wouldn't let me go
ever again, till death parted us. She sounded insane, she was
screeching. She'd been adopted by a family in the police and
now she wanted to know why I'd abandoned her. I didn't ask
her in because she was threatening me, she kept saying: You
slut, you'll pay for this, I want money, I'll never leave you in
peace ever again. She was laughing and crying all at once,
waving at the sky to show me that there was my witness and
my judge, that she'd have her revenge. I thought I was in a
nightmare but no, it was true, she really was my daughter.
Agnès. I chose that name—it was my doll's name, I didn't
look far for that one. Now she's back every day, harassing
me, the last month of my life has been unrecognizable.
Just last week I got another text message, she wrote, look
I haven't deleted it: "I'm going to kill you, slut." She kept
on copying the same text to me, I got it twenty-six times,
I think perhaps her phone had a fault, there was a glitch

anyway. I had to make a formal complaint. So this is my life. I'm completely exhausted. I don't know what to do, I can't sleep, I'm mortally afraid, my life is shot to pieces. And my children know nothing of my past. I wanted to explain it in a little private book, I don't want to just say it to them like this, I'd like to give them written words. A book is precious; that's why I thought of you.

The muezzin's call to prayer sounds over Madame Henry's voice, I let her fade away and the colors of the village return, I still have memories to stow, I must organize my belongings, the night will be long, it's still a child as they say in Lisbon. I didn't see Madame Henry again, she had something of Emma Bovary about her, I didn't even call her the following day to say no, Louise, forgive me, I cannot write this book, and although your story moves me deeply I know I wouldn't have either the strength or the right to set it down: again, forgive me. For a few moments, I saw her twenty years earlier, talking passionately about Julien, I recalled her muslin blouses, her moccasins, her perfume, her big gestures. We had gone together to Lyons-la-Forêt and Ry to see them shoot the Claude Chabrol film; it was she who had told me about it, saying that the two villages would be in the movies and all the villagers would have parts, we can't miss this, she'd said on the phone, come quick, the film crew will be around all week and Isabelle Huppert is playing Emma, what fun! I knew that Lyons-la-Forêt and Ry each claimed the laurel as the setting for Flaubert's novel. At Lyons-la-Forêt they shrugged and said that of course

Yonville-L'Abbaye *was* Lyons, Flaubert had been inspired by every last detail of the village and especially by its superb great house, Ry was just a little local spot while Lyons was something special, you had only to look, no call for photos. At Ry they said you could easily recreate a map of Yonville simply by reversing the map of Ry, you could even see the path Madame Bovary used to take every day: she'd go this way and then she'd turn there to come out at the church, what's more you can see her grave by the porch, it says Delphine Delamare but it's actually Emma Bovary's, Charles's wife. The scenes of every chapter in the novel are all around here: on the near side of the bridge, in the old cider press, at the automata museum, you can see Rodolphe, Léon, Charles, Homais, and even little Berthe brought back to life, and at the end of your visit, you understand what really happened. Chabrol was recording conversations with everyone, accepting, never judging, he savored every observation, and he had indeed hired all the residents to appear in the film as extras. The pharmacist, the baker, the antiques dealer, the *charcutière*, the watchmaker, the ironmonger— everyone was there in costume, strolling in the streets of Lyons and Ry, it was great fun, Madame Henry was right. You could go and talk to Chabrol between takes, he'd be sitting beside the camera, very calm, leafing through magazines, always ready to answer the locals' questions. He knew every version of the novel, he'd rummaged in the archives in Rouen, he had even dug out Flaubert's preparatory sketches toward certain scenes, his working method, his manuscripts, his rough drafts, his letters to Louise Colet, which alone were a treasure trove: It's a feast, he'd say. And you know, Flaubert is very coarse in his drafts, much more than in the novel, he writes of their "screw" in the carriage, of Emma and Léon using "tongues" and, describing Emma, he draws her like this—and it's deliciously rude: "She returns to Yonville in the happy physical state that follows everyday fucking, it was jam-making season." So we see he clearly took great pleasure in writing this masterpiece, and for me it was a genuine challenge to retain his style in my film. Laughing on the porch of the church at Ry, Chabrol had even discussed his first encounter with the novel at age thirteen or fourteen, on the eve of his first time, in the forest, with his young girlfriend: I don't know if it had anything to do with it, but both things happened at almost the same moment.

Looking out to sea, I raise my glass to Flaubert, to Chabrol, and to Madame Henry—I think I'm missing her a little. And Mathilde, will I miss her when I can't see her anymore? She doesn't know yet that I'm leaving; when to tell her?

Very slowly, I drink my glass of muscat. So many images in just a few seconds. With each sip the throbbing of even more invisible hearts joins me, moments of a life, reflections of light on a face, the scars of hours, culled from the past or perhaps still unknown, thousands of sparks dissolved in my every breath. Hearts in thrall drawing together. Geraniums, pink and white carnations, the unfurling leaves of bougain-villea, odd fragments of broken pots, pieces of colored glass, fraying fabrics, linen sheets, pebbles, everyday conversations. Conversations at the café, on a train, on the beach, at the market, from one terrace to another, or beside the dried fruit kiosk. It's almost always the most fleeting figures who return and ask to come in, to sit down, to stop for a glass of something and talk. In this house—how to describe it?—I have a bird's-eye view of every period of my life, everything reappears whole, everything fits back into place, even the years I never knew, even the very briefest moments, objects forgotten or passed over too cursorily, even the thrills and the anxieties. There is something magical here; it is what binds me to the house as if to a great love. This is why I keep coming back to it. To look after everything that will come to me here. This, too, is why leaving it tears me apart, as much as leaving the country. This morning, on the bakery terrace in La Marsa, I was the only customer. I asked for my coffee "direct," which means with a drop of milk just to cut the bitterness, I sat and stared at the ground, I couldn't tear my thoughts away from yesterday's attack and Alain's death, everything had become so unreal over the last few months, since *Charlie Hebdo*, but doubtless since much earlier still. Since the assassination of Daniel Pearl, who had been forced to say I am Jewish my father is Jewish my mother is Jewish, before he'd been beheaded and his body hacked into ten pieces. Then there had been Ilan Halimi, how could we forget? Then Mohamed Merah. And now, not a moment's respite. But it's impossible and entirely pointless to put a date to this death machine, the violence is gaining pace, the threat is growing for everyone, we must get used to it, we keep on saying, our arguments go around in circles, no more words, no more strength. The waiter too looked downcast, he might have been reading the images silently revolving in my head. There wasn't a car on the road, the florist was closed, no one in the local park either, a country suddenly abandoned, ravaged, and I too ravaged. Shame has taken hold. The failure of what no one now dares to call "the rev-olution." And yet, on so many faces, you could still read not only the desire for it but the knowledge of their difference, of belief in a model country where politics and religion would be kept apart, which would gradually be strengthening its democracy, which would protect its constitution. And we always took heart at that old refrain, and it was everywhere to be heard: freedom must be conquered, she cannot be easily won; it will take time but we will get there; we have toppled a dictator, the aim was to be better off, not worse. But again and again, assassinations and bombings smash and scatter that confidence, each time impoverishing and grinding the country down a little lower.

At one point, the waiter came up to me, he wiped the table with a sponge and said shyly that it was very bad what had happened yesterday, that we had no right to hurt tourists, that the guy must have been a madman, but all the same life had gotten too expensive, wages weren't going up, you couldn't even buy medicines anymore, that's why some of the young people were getting up to no good, they'd given up on the government, they didn't even have money to take to the market, before you could buy everything for five *dinars*, now you pay ten times as much and your basket's still empty. They say they prefer to throw their lives away with a suicide belt than live in poverty, I don't know where they picked that up, it's not in the Qu'ran, they've been brainwashed, that's for sure. And it's worse in the South, they're completely off the radar, one day it'll explode, it has to. The young people should be told to keep working and studying to build up the country instead of going to Syria or Libya, we have to go to the villages and bring them work, it's even worse in the villages, you'd think the government has abandoned the people there. But we can't give up, otherwise we'll all die like they did yesterday and we don't want to die, we love life too much, that's just how Tunisians are, we've always loved life, everyone knows that. I was trying to listen but his reasoning was so disarming that I couldn't reply, I hadn't the heart. Then he touched my hand and his face lit up with a remarkable smile: Am I right or aren't I?

Yes, Slim, you're right, I said. I was dazzled by the transformation in his face. Suddenly he'd smiled just like the tiny Cairene girl in the City of the Dead all that time ago, I had forgotten to ask her name but her smile had lasted through the years, had become almost sacred to me. Those seconds in which one face can show the sum of an entire community's ordeal. A single face, open, defenseless, that awakens, that summons and thereby conveys the heart of a whole country. Those two faces shared the same radiance and I was stunned. The little girl wears a torn red skirt and a lime green T-shirt, her hair is tangled but very shiny, great ringlets of it down to her waist. She is weeping beside a tomb that serves both as her playground and her house, she's been hurt by a stone, blood trickles from her hand, she is alone, maybe four years old, she holds her hand up to the sky and she weeps. I edge in between the tombs, searingly hot in the sun, I approach her, I take out a tissue, show it to her, and sprinkle it with perfume, I bandage it around her thumb. She stops weeping, follows my movements one by one, she doesn't understand that someone could come and see her injury and try to look after her. She looks at me without speaking and little by little, she grows calm, her smile takes shape, it rises into her eyes and illuminates her completely, a true joy for both of us; she shows me the wreck of an old pool table on the far side of the tombs and asks me to play with her. Her face has stayed with me, stored away, after so many years it hasn't shifted, then it slipped into Slim's face to be revealed once more: the tears, those wide eyes, the little injured hand, the red skirt, the light of her smile, and the two of us in the midst of that graveyard-town, with the rainbow colors of the clothes drying on the tombs, the saucepans and frying pans, the spinning tops and empty pickling jars all around us, and beyond all this, the vast city, its dilapidated blocks, savage slums, the honking and the dust, the makeshift open-air beds on roof terraces, high up where the birds and minarets call to each other, overlay, chime together, and dizzy me, then mingle with the call of Sidi-Bou-Saïd's muezzin, there, close by, just now as I write.

On that trip to Cairo, Jacques Hassoun had wanted to show me the prison in the Citadel where he'd been held for six months in 1953, before leaving the country a year later. He was born in Alexandria and you could pick out the colors of Egypt in his Parisian psychoanalyst's study: between his old books, pots, jewelry, and paintings, Egypt hadn't left him. Hundreds of prisoners' arms rushed out between bars and gestured to us; from some distance away we could hear the terrible screams of people we couldn't see: It was exactly the same when I was there, it's incredible, Jacques had said, quite relaxed in the midst of the crowd, the filth, and the dust. I couldn't joke about it as he did, I was petrified. But he quickly explained that actually these were not screams of distress, it was just visiting hour, the prisoners had to shout in order to be heard by those who gathered in rows beneath their windows. Look, a visitor stands beneath each window because they're not allowed to go up and see them. They were just asking for news of their mother, their son, their father, or for the paper they needed. That day the intense heat in addition to the violence of these scenes had overwhelmed me and I also couldn't get used to the escort assigned to us as we moved around the country; it was rumored that some attacks were imminent and the police who surrounded us each time we made a trip were on edge. I thought again of the Jews' great exodus from the Muslim countries, all at about the same moment, around 1956, then more and more, with each big political crisis, through to 1967, and even though it might have been possible to go on living together in spite of everything, I could sense that I must be one of the last still to hope for that, so I said nothing, I stared at the dust, I let myself disappear among the prisoners' screams, I was nowhere, the glorious image of my parents stepping out of the great theater one winter evening flashed briefly past but the dust covered it all again almost immediately.

Come, stop daydreaming, let's go, it's time to find ourselves some tasty fava bean stew, Jacques said. Buoyed up by this return to his native land, he wanted to see everything at once, experience everything afresh, taste everything, his youth and all the sensations he wanted to feel in just a few hours, he was speaking rapidly, at once telling the history of the different quarters and that of the old texts, he was magnificent, I tried to keep up with his excitement but it wasn't easy. I knew too that his delight and impatience masked a profound melancholy and a wound that nothing could heal. Jacques' book *L'Exil de la langue* was one of my favorites, I reread it frequently in order to understand my own history. In the book he tries to rediscover the substance of that secret language carried with us in the only suitcase we could never lose: our hearts. A language in which we'd lived as children but that we'd never been taught. From there he picked out particular connections between the minority speaker and the language of power, between memory and forgetting; he said that our past experiences could become tools for survival. In his eyes flickered something unresolved, he was at once smiling and on the verge of tears. Consequently he had taken me, along with some other friends also born in Egypt but who hadn't returned till then, to visit one of the city's oldest synagogues. They had opened it for our group and Jacques had tried to lead a prayer inside that vast empty space: the Friday service. But just when it came to the singing, he had lost his voice, with each word he grew hoarser, and he finished in a barely audible whisper. He was as surprised as we were by this phenomenon but he went on, he sang the service right to the end. No one said a word, we pretended everything had gone well, we didn't want to spoil the trip nor puncture his high spirits, but sadness, weariness, and melancholy had suddenly engulfed us all.

The years, faces, objects crowd over each other and dazzle me again.

My father is walking down the Avenue in a fine white cotton shirt, a panama on his head, he is twenty-seven, he walks with great elegance, he knows that this city belongs to him, his scent floats all the way back to me, it's Pompeia by Piver. A crate of glossy green figs on the Hammamet road, they're bursting open, stuffed with sweetness, their tiny seeds so red and gleaming inside; it's Sunday, a black Peugeot stops, the crate is sold, the exhaust gives a great belch, leaves a black trail through the village behind it, and the Peugeot turns left, toward the beach: children's hands wave from the window to say watch out, we're turning! You can hear the children's shouts far out on the road, even after the car has vanished in a black cloud. The long and almost deserted beach awaits them, they'll drive onto the sand and right down to the sea, which is so clear they'll see the shoals of fish in the green water, fat black inner tubes will be their floats, and now great backward somersaults, noses tightly clutched. A gray kitten is watching me, mournfully; he's my adopted pet, he's dying of typhoid, he asks me for help, I give him a little milk but after two sucks he stops, he can't swallow it, I stroke him until his last breath, and he doesn't stop looking at me, he is pleading, then he drops onto one side, such a thin body, he drops and already he is stiff. I don't understand what's happened, I talk to him, I say come, my little Rio Bravo, open your eyes, please, don't leave me, I'm here. He doesn't respond. High summer is all around us. I wrap him in newspaper and go to bury him in the straggly bushes near the train tracks. No one has seen me, I'm eight and a half, I hold onto my tears so they can't fall, it's siesta hour, I don't tell anyone what happened, it's so hot at this time in the afternoon, it's burning my feet, I've gone out barefoot, I learned all alone how we can die in the space of a second.

A powder-puff scent traverses and marks time through the seasons; so familiar. Wearing her pink silk dress, my mother hums "Tintarella di luna," she's so graceful in this late afternoon light. Gino the Neapolitan hairdresser from rue de Marseille is at the door, he has Pento cream in his tightly curled hair, his white linen pants are spotless, he says goodbye, see you soon, Bice dear; the starlings in the Avenue's fig trees strike up their evening concert and the whole city sings with possibility, if you look to the left you can see that the soldier on guard in front of the General's Residence remains stock still in his little white wood cabin, he never tires. The flamingos skim over the Lake of Tunis, making pink lines across the sky, the smell is abominable but the view is magnificent, it takes in the very fabric of the road, the sky, the tarmac, grains of sand stuck between our toes until the next trip to the beach, and over there the profile of the great liner *El Djezaïr* that has just docked from Marseille, it's the big ship's moment: hands lift and wave along the quay, others standing on the ship's bridge wave in answer, on the one side floral dresses, on the other thick woollen coats, everyone has spotted everyone else, nothing but colors everywhere and joy, the wait has been so long. Jerry Lewis and Dean Martin are embracing in a red convertible, the one man grimacing and contorted with a clownish look on his face, the other smiling, his arms caress the air and he sings like the crooner he is.

The screen at the Palmarium is hung with red velvet drapes and speaks to us of glorious America, it teaches us to dream. The smell of disinfectant taints whole years, focuses each image, flows back and forth between the watchers'

dazzled faces and those of the stars gesticulating in their overwrought scenes. Rock Hudson, Clark Gable, Shirley MacLaine, Burt Lancaster, Natalie Wood, David Niven, Doris Day, James Mason, Ava Gardner. On the screen now, a bowl of spaghetti slips out of Jerry Lewis's hands, the whole cinema erupts and instantly adopts the line "scared stiff," then joyfully broadcasts it into the city's streets for any occasion someone shows the least sign of fright. The camera's white beam extends a long corridor of dust so mobile and alive that we watch it as much as the film, everything in that unique combination of smells, disinfectant, and roasted peanuts, to recall that once Tunis really was a "Cinema City" with a hundred theaters to its name.

In the physics and chemistry lecture theater, Monsieur Béhar tops off his test tubes. He wears a white coat, he is our wizard, teaching us the complexities and secrets of the formulae; later in Paris, with the same minute care, he would give me the recipe for a delicious honey and almond cake, to be cut into little squares and doused in orange flower–infused syrup.

Outside in the Lycée Carnot's courtyard, the swifts are waiting for our sweet brioches to come out, they swoop to and fro above the terraces, winter is mild in these parts. Biribi, the true magician, sets up in our classrooms every year a few days before Christmas, he makes fluorescent scarves appear and two white rabbits pop out of his top hat. He gives me the shivers, I hide behind Marie-Thérèse Grillo and in short order I've caught one of the poppy-flavored hard candies that he shares out among us before he goes: A joyful Christmas to you, children! On the first day of spring, Marie-Thérèse comes to show us her extraordinary white confirmation dress, and her cross and gold earrings. We cheer her with all our strength, she's so beautiful and, for days afterward, I dream of that wedding dress, I ask my mother if I too, one day.

Those shots from *Night and Fog* appear once more before my eyes that will not close again, there's no recovering from what they've seen, for the first time I wonder if I'm part of a we, if I too could have been one of those lifeless bodies, my eyes keep their counsel on the path to the house, this house almost adjoining the synagogue, I carry this film in my body for ever after, even when it's time to go, to leave the house. It reappears at the most unexpected moments, at moments of love, moments of joy or fear, something terrible will happen to us for sure, and without warning. Stopping at the building's cast-iron bars I look furtively in at the synagogue and consider what it means to live so close to it, to sleep with its great body there, so nearby. I look and question it in silence, as if seeing it for the first time, or rather as if I'm no longer the same person. And when I see the film again, many years later, straight away, over the heaps of objects, hair, watches, and bodies, my mind superimposes memories of those great gatherings we used to watch from the balcony, all those families clustered beneath blue-and-white striped shawls on the Day of Atonement. Solemn, inward-looking faces, heads bent beneath the fine linen cloth, and wordless, they looked so sure of where they stood, on the steps of this synagogue nowadays fallen almost silent, under constant armed surveillance and surrounded by barbed wire. The name Daniel Iffla Osiris remains discreetly associated with the place.

Memory in pieces, scattered pieces to be reassembled patiently, to attempt to understand. Or again those long parades of menorahs that trailed right across the town to finish at the synagogue, I've forgotten the name of that holy day, I think we used simply to call it the feast of the flowers. Every child in new clothes, holding a candle entwined with fresh flowers, walking very upright so as to not let the flickering flame blow out, staring at it as if only the power of that stare, unwavering even for a second, could keep it both alive and lively. Flames so mobile, so delicate, lighting great lines along the sidewalks, slowly they'd come down both sides of the Avenue, flames so naïve that I could weep today: How to picture that, in a Muslim country, all those Jewish families used to calmly, from each season to the next, reenact their ancient rites, like that, without the least concern, almost lightly, without really believing in it, and above all with such confidence? How to explain that it was precisely this amalgamation of cultures that gave the country its unique bedrock?

The synagogue had been consecrated on December 23, 1937, my mother was seven months pregnant, she had followed the progress of the construction from her balcony, she was impatient. Her first-born son would bear the name of the prophet Elias because he had appeared to her in a dream and announced the coming of a boy. In her dream, the prophet had even suggested she call him Elias, she had said yes, why not, I'll do it, I promise, but it'll be his second name, I do so want to call him Claude. She always came to reasonable accommodation with the ineffable. The prophet Elias had kept his promise and she had too: my brother was born at the very beginning of March 1938, and his second name is indeed Eliaou. In 1942 when she was pregnant with her third child, the Germans occupied the synagogue, she watched them come and go from her balcony, they chatted on the steps in their frightening uniforms, she kept a hand on her belly, she wanted to protect all her children, she closed the shutters and went to listen to the news on Radio Londres. If I stare now at the steps of that synagogue, this is what I see. One morning many years later, my father asked me to wait for him there, on those steps, he'd be there in a minute, he always used the same expression: I'll come and go. He never said I'll come back, and we didn't dare correct him, we loved him as he was, with all his mistakes and his overlavish kindness. His brother Léon was waiting for him on the other side of the road. I was not to cross with him, I was to stay there and not move. I never spoke to this uncle, my father seemed to be ashamed of him. He was short, poorly dressed, poorly shaved, his arms dangled, he looked like a tramp. My father dug his hand into his pants pocket, took out some loose bills, and gave them to his brother. Léon inspected them, said thank you, and went, his eyes on the ground at first, arms held stiffly at his sides, then suddenly looking up and pointedly ahead. The same scene recurred three or four times. Always on the same spot Léon appeared, and my father disbursed also always at the same place. I watched them do this, understanding nothing, asking no questions, only uneasy. A long time later, I learned that this uncle had inherited my grandfather's little jewelry shop but hadn't known how to sustain it, that little by little it had failed and he'd ruined his family by betting on the horses at Kassar-Saïd. Very soon he had nothing left at all, his wife was dead and his children had rejected him, expelled him from the house. But there was something else too. Léon liked boys and perhaps also young girls, this I learned later still, the day of his death, but there was nothing to be done, that's how he was, better to look the other way, so my father had said. He alone of the family continued to give the man a little money, but he absolutely would not have his children approach or talk to him.

All around the synagogue, there's the little life of the neighborhood, buried deep these days, but if I go that way, I always wear my archaeologist's sun hat and it's not hard to dig up. The smell of the Davin laundry, that of the magazines imported from France, of the violet-flavored hard candies in the little shop next door. Farther on, if you turn left into rue Randon, the one-eyed grocer shapes little blue paper cones to weigh the sugar and flour, *carta da zucchero* blue, that paper, a very pale powder blue. The Chemouni brothers' old-fashioned "Roman" scale sits shining on the high, polished-wood counter, it sits waiting in shadow, it knows every client's name. The terribly thin toasted-linseed seller stands at the corner of the rue Hoche in an old threadbare red sweater; over his call, a single word that he repeats endlessly all day long, there now rattles the noise of the two tramlines that meet on the avenue: it's at this moment that my father goes by, a panama on his head and in a fine fresh white shirt, he's a young married man, only twenty-seven, my mother is waiting for him on the balcony, he smiles to her, he's bringing her delicious sugar-coated pistachios, he waves the see-through packet to show her: his Béatrice, he so admires her, she's beautiful and cultivated, she's his princess and they have a fine family to bring into the world.

"I like this part of the country; I am fond of living here because I am attached to it by deep roots, the profound and delicate roots that attach a man to the soil on which his ancestors were born and died, to their traditions, their usages, their food, the local expressions, the peculiar language of the peasants, the smell of the soil, the hamlets, and to the atmosphere itself." These are Maupassant's words in *The Horla*, a novella my mother bought for me at Kessis, the little stationer on the Avenue de Paris. Maupassant's books frighten even while they enchant me; I read them too early, too much violence for a child of eleven or twelve, but my mother had no sense of timing, she would give me the books she liked as one offers a child food—and I would take them, with thanks, and discover their worlds. It was love she was offering me in these books and I needed her love. In fact, the books stood in for what she couldn't otherwise give, being too taken up with her own anxiety and quite at a loss when it came to her children and the rest of life. So she would read, she'd play the piano, she embroidered, made chocolate cakes, told us secrets, and then, when she had run through all her crafts, she would throw it all out in a temper for it was quite clear to her that she lacked one, the most valuable of all: she wanted love and that she did not have. Before foundering with this lack of love, she used to talk to us of it in her own way. She used to say that she was in love with love but that it was invisible. We used to listen to her, we tried to understand. She would tell us the stories of her favorite novels and films, of Rita Hayworth's pearl necklace in *Separate Tables* and Kim Novak's chignon in *Vertigo*. The story of *Pandora* delighted her, that absolute love that could endure for centuries, along with the legend of the *Flying Dutchman*, of the man who killed the woman he loved, believing her to be unfaithful, and who was punished, condemned to wander the seas for eternity without ever being able to die. She would close her eyes in ecstasy as she told these tales. Ava Gardner was one of her idols, a princess,

she called her, you must see how she swims through the
darkness toward the boat, how beautiful she is with her wet
hair, how she tosses her head back in the water, like this,
and raises it again to show her spectacular beauty, she's unforgettable, that woman; she swims in silence through the
sparkling black water because she's sure someone will be
waiting for her there, on the boat, and that it will be her
true love. And she does find him: it's James Mason. And
he happens to be painting the portrait of a woman just like
her, the face of she who haunts him ever since his crime, he
paints her though he doesn't yet know her, that film is so,
so beautiful, I can't tell you the whole thing, you have to see
it. She was so happy in those moments, she promised we
would see *Pandora and the Flying Dutchman* as soon as it
showed again in Tunis. James Mason, she would say, laughing, there's a man I could have married, so handsome, such
intense eyes and his face always a little sad, my kind of man
I tell you, perhaps not exactly him but a man just like him.
She could have run out onto her balcony and wailed to the
people below that she was wasting away for love, that her
heart was truly in pain for lack of it, but no, she confided
only in us and then somehow, at the least little annoyance,
a mistake, something misplaced, a concern about nothing
at all, or waiting for one of her children who was dallying
on the way back from school, and it was over. I had a terrible fright, she would say. Or sometimes: I've had a shock.
And she would tap her chest, that's where it all went on,
a place where anything could happen without warning, a
place where she had no control, where long-forgotten losses
might reemerge, and then she would say no more at all, she
let go of her body, her gaze fell to the floor, it was hopeless.

It would come on rapidly, within about two days, two days of uncertainty during which we tried to read her every movement: she'd be poised between two moods, between brilliance and anguish. Then, every time, she would go under altogether, she'd be in bed all day long, weeping, drinking nothing but milk, smoking cigarette after cigarette, wanting to die. The cycle of misery was begun again. At these times, books were my lifeline. Through them, I found a mother who was always happy, always playful, ready for new adventures. They took care of me and gave me joy, I became attached to them; their presence was real and they fed me with confidence, they held an invisible potency that I gulped down. Maupassant's books and, later, Flaubert's settled in the house like friendly souls, they made me want to see these Normandy farmlands, their forests, their tortured souls, shaped by the earth, by prejudice and mud: even while disquieting and stirring me, they kept me alert, made me want to live passionately. They exposed people's fragility, the ease with which we can be broken by a single blow, go mad or turn criminal, break the rules and get drunk on it. More than any other, the main character in *The Horla* fascinated me. I would read and reread that book, trying to understand it better; sometimes I thought I got close, like him I heard strange noises in the house, a menacing presence that never left me, I never knew if it was distant or right beside me, within or without, was someone perhaps coming to kill all of us, at once? I followed the protagonist through to the torching of his house and his inexorable death, I watched the fire he had lit hoping thereby to rid himself of his malevolent double, and I wondered how in so few pages this man had been brought down. Everything happened so fast, nothing showed of his disturbance in the opening lines, yet within a few days he had become possessed: How was this possible, what had happened to him?

And yet I could understand the metamorphosis, for my mother too had several faces, she switched from one to another without warning, something inside her regularly wrested control and assailed her whole being. I stood witness to this war. I couldn't help her, only take her arm, soothe her, make up songs for her and, more than anything, work hard, never make myself a burden. I read and reread, I so ached to see the Normandy that lived in these pages, I could already make out the landscape around Rouen, the Etretat cliffs, Dieppe, Le Tréport, I'd have liked to walk their pebbles, all these lands that had grown so dear to me: one day perhaps, who could tell?

When, later, I did come to the villages of Haute-Normandie, now and then I seemed to catch Maupassant's voice again, or that of Barbey d'Aurevilly, when he wrote: "Literature does not relate half the crimes that society commits mysteriously and with impunity every day, with delightful frequency and facility." But most of all and almost everywhere I stumbled upon Flaubert. His characters lived on, they seemed to be right there, standing just outside my gate, I had only to welcome them in. Lyons-la-Forêt, Ry, the tiny roads of the Andelle valley, the dreams and nightmares secreted in the depths of those copses, the animal tracks through the forest, the screech owls' cries at three in the morning, deer glimpsed in the undergrowth: almost a hallucination so swift was their transit. And the crimes: that of a days-old baby discovered drowned in the Andelle, and that of young Alexandre who was killed by two bullets to the back of his neck, then burned by his four best friends, there, right in front of my house, four years ago, on the Vierge-Marie path. He was seventeen, his friends a little younger, two sets of brothers.

I have also loved and still love this land that is Tunisia, with a strange and powerful love. I love the city of Tunis, the Carthage coast, La Marsa, Gammarth, the little villages of the South, the complexity of this society, the ever-present confrontation between the dispossessed and the super-wealthy, this country that might split at the seams from one day to the next, like a person, a land that's searing and sweet at the same time. I love to trace its history, it is unique in the Arab world, it could lead the way. But there's something else that gnaws at me: this question of not truly knowing why I love it so deeply. Always I stumble at this love: I don't understand it. I'd like to explain it better for myself. I don't believe it's because I was born here, nor due to "the profound and delicate roots that attach a man to the soil on which his ancestors were born and died"—no, I've never harked back to my childhood years, rather they felt quite a burden, my mother's illness swallowed us up along with her, and it took great energy to overcome all those hours of distress read upon her face, day after day, so hard to forget. Leaving for Paris, I thought, meant leaving that childhood behind forever, I set sail lighthearted and confident: to not look back, to see the world, there was so, so much to learn, the years that scrolled out ahead expectantly seemed inexhaustible, I was jubilant, to dance through life was my motto and I too was in love with love. Why, then, have I come back so often? Why, in the end, despite how things look, have I found it so hard to break away, as my parents and family have done, I mean completely? My father never talked about this rupture. He came to Paris when he was sixty-one, a few months after my mother, abandoning the country where his ancestors had lived for centuries. Within a few months, he had to join his children in France, he had to abandon his life, his profession, his house, his habits, his music, his landscape, and above all his shop, which was his whole life, as he used to say. Not a word of this vital rupture, never a complaint, either from him or my mother. They both still wore the same shy smiles, so as not to trouble anyone, or lean on anyone, even when they were not all right at all, charming smiles that still make me shiver today. This is the story of so many exiles, of all those who today cross the Mediterranean and die at sea, in their thousands they go, are lost in their thousands, their story is ours too, it tugs at our hearts. For my parents of course, it was quite different: they had wanted to move to France and had already adopted it so much earlier, in their language and culture. They knew, even without much political education, that it was France that had broadly ensured their safety and dignity for all these years, even if it hadn't all been perfect. But the deep, wordless wound of having left their country so brutally, as if it were a natural step: this they kept in silence, folded deep inside, like so many others, not daring to touch on or venture near it; and this I meant to feel in my turn. They had wordlessly passed it down to me, it had become my wound. And perhaps, after all, it was this that I'd sought to treat by returning, by trying to recover their childhood, by recreating what they saw through the long years they lived between Tunis and La Marsa. The Protectorate, beylic life, the move from out-of-the-way districts to the European city that was built in less than thirty years. The world war, the fear of the Germans' preparations toward great rounds of arrests in their quarter, the tensions between communities, the administrative hassles, the unjust imprisonments, the small but regular humiliations. Independence and Tunisians' gradual resumption of their country, the national holidays, the street names that changed, flags too. Then the political crises, the nationalizations, the delicate balance of power. The Six-Day War; sudden chaos. And finally, departure. Of course, I also wanted to relive their joys, the parties, the delights of summer, their hopes, their distresses, the ways they understood and, by hook or by crook, fashioned their lives within a society both cosmopolitan and traditional, both modern and riddled with superstition, prejudice, and ancient obstructions. How had they managed to throw off this burden of inheritance; how had they spared us the encumbrance? And more than anything, how were they able to bear leaving it all behind, forever? It seemed I needed to see places again, to maintain some connection, to be there. Now they're dead, I feel the only way I can still console them is by writing. Knowing that in spite of everything I will recapture nothing, for this time it's really over: I too must go, must leave those I love, perhaps never to return, I don't know yet. I could, like so many others, have looked on this land from afar, like a utopia, an idealized, sugar-dusted country, and never set foot here again, understanding that there was no longer a place here for the "foreigners" we had become since choosing France.

I could, by lying to myself, have kept this land cozily stored in memories and turned to it from time to time for flashes of what I'd have called moments of truth or moments of happiness, while automatically repeating that we used to live so happily all together. I didn't do it. Because that would have been to lie: we did not live so happily all together, we lived side by side, we tolerated each other, we probably liked each other, but only up to a point, up to a point and no further. It's this line that I have sought to cross by continually returning, with each visit however brief, by loving what the country has become today, by keeping watch over its struggles and hopes, by being there, by forging new friendships, loving, deeply felt friendships, by keeping confidence.

I think mainly that I wanted to go on being there for my father: to put myself in his position, to see through his eyes. To set down a few words about the rupture that he'd tried to minimize. To reconnect with what was wrested from him and what he had to abandon. I came back because I wanted to be, mere handful that we are, among the last to return and tirelessly to observe this land, I wanted to set my feet back in the paths of the departed, come back to what they left in the city, in the very fabric of the landscapes and the air, to talk with the thousands of names buried in the Borgel cemetery, to read the love poems inscribed in the tombs' stone slabs, to stare at the hundred-year-old eucalyptus trees that were already there, guarding the same turns, when my parents were children and used to play among the ruins of Carthage and on the beach at La Marsa. The smells, the colors, the movements, the sensations that they had gathered and then left behind, I wanted to capture them, to set them in motion once more, to broadcast them. Ways of seasoning a dish, of speaking and thinking at lightning speed, of savoring the briefest moment's pleasure, of sighing, of bursting into laughter right after sighing and thinking themselves in heaven just then—yes, I wanted to feel all of this again, to feel it for them, to affirm there is still space for them. I particularly wanted to do this in the real world, with today's Tunisians, through all those to whom I've grown attached, not only through my memories. And I wanted to do it for them, to offer them our memories so they can restore our lives to the life of their country. I'm only a fragment, a single piece plucked from a shared history; not to come back would have been to admit that I accepted the total abandonment of our history. The temptation to do this remains strong, for I do feel that I've become a stranger in this country, that my life is in France and that it's very far removed from what I see and hear here, but the task I have set myself cannot be dropped now. Even backbreaking as it has become.

Yet this evening, for the first time, I too call a pause. There is a fight for softness, Barthes said. This is the struggle that I, in my turn, take up. Too much violence for anyone to confront, our wounds are too fresh. Yesterday, on arriving at the beach, the boy who killed the tourists at El Kantaoui told the Tunisians bathing nearby not to be afraid, he wasn't going to kill *them*, only the others, he said, only the foreigners. I can't get that scene or those words out of my head, this attack marks the limits of what I can bear, and this is why I want both to leave and to bear witness to my love. I know that beach so well, the gestures of the tourists who were there, of those who'd just arrived and those who perhaps having already stayed a week would be returning home that evening. I know the mystery of all the grains of sand, the white, the gray, the black, and the transparent. The strips of seaweed, cigarette butts, soda bottle caps, giant ants, peanut shells. The deck chairs, yellow-and-white striped towels, suntan oil, sunglasses, the books still with a few grains of sand wedged inside. The lemonade set on a low table, a few coins beside it, cellphones. The smell of salt on your clothes, eyes closed against the bright sky, picking up conversations all around, the skin pearly and tender. I know everything of these bodies stretched out in the sun, here to experience this beach for the first time; I am a piece of these bodies. A single whisper of death and it's all gone. Now the bodies on the sand are covered by the yellow and white towels, some strips of swimsuits still showing, feet, a hand, text messages race up the cellphone screens, unanswered. A single whisper and everything can vanish? That nagging anxiety that used to envelop me as a child, at the Café Vert, and regularly gripped me during the night, resounds now, deafeningly, through this scene. I am speechless, revolted, petrified, scandalized. Would every thought, then, however fleeting, one day take shape and be played out even far away, anywhere, transformed into real-life action, unimaginable to that point? The formless threat that I have anticipated since early childhood yesterday took the shape of forty minutes of terror on the beach at Sousse, by El Kantaoui port. It happened, and it happened here: guests have been killed because they were guests. On the day before he died, my father had lunch at my house and asked me to give him my book— it was my first novel, it had just been published. I didn't dare, I didn't want to shock him: I said I had no more copies but that next time I would give him one, specially for him, I promised. I was standing in the doorway and he already on the stairs, he held up a finger and said again: Really, next time, you'll give me one? You won't forget me, I'm still your father after all? I said yes, I promise. And I blew him a kiss.

The next day, he was found dead in his car, the police called me to say that it was his heart and if I wanted to see him, I could come to the mortuary. It has taken me many years to resolve to write it, the book I promised him and that I was meant to give him, the book specially for him, to tell him that no, I would not forget him.

This evening, before leaving, I will finish it, the book, in this enchanted house that has a body, a scent, and a heart. More and more its light resembles that long-running old dream that faithfully accompanied my nights for so many years, I recognize it. So I will finish the book in this house in Sidi-Bou-Saïd, the village he loved to return to when he used to bring us along: he loved the summer nights, after the open-air cinema in Kram, loved to buy a jasmine sprig and tuck it behind his ear, loved to have tea with pine nuts at the café on the corner, the café downstairs as he liked to call it; the blue-painted steel chairs are still there and the tea served in glasses. But not the great mosque, that wasn't yet built; that's where he used to park his Peugeot 404, on the empty lot beside the overgrown garden. Back then, only the mosque stood high against the sky, with its minaret that looked like a church spire; we knew that it harbored Saint Bou Saïd's mausoleum and that the great courtyard looked out over the bay and Bou-Kornine, a glorious view. We never went up to the top of the village, the rumor went that it was a holy village and only wise men and poets could go there, it was forbidden to us, or at least we refused to go up there, preferring to look at it from below and see it appear gradually, from the road that runs from Carthage and Amilcar. The spotless white and blue of the houses was much admired,

their gentle geometry, the violet bougainvillea that over-
flowed the villa walls, and the mosque directly above the
café, like a watchman, stationed between the heavens and
the mazy alleyways. The architecture was perfect, the village
looked like a prince born of a dream of peace, an Eastern
dream: our dream.

Facing this sea—my father's sea, I am writing my farewell to the country, and I present this farewell to him, to honor my promise. I present it too to all those who, like him, held their tongues, thinking to protect their children. All those who kept their suffering hidden away inside, who pretended it was easy to go, to leave all that they'd built, slowly, generation upon generation. One day, in Paris, he wanted to see me urgently, he had something very important to say. I said come, we'll have coffee, it's been too long since you came to the house, almost a month. The last time I'd seen him, he'd invited me to a wedding in Porte Maillot to introduce me to a man who would, he said, be a very good match for me. He'd always loved that phrase: a good match. But, *Papa*, I'm not alone, we have a child and we're doing well, I'm really not about to marry this man I don't even know! I was thirty, our daughter was three, Baptiste was an actor, my father didn't consider that a real profession, not secure enough. Yes, yes, I know, your boyfriend is nice but even so, you never know, you'd have no anxieties with this one and I'd be happier too, I'm worried about your future, you know, he's a top doctor, you wouldn't have this hand-to-mouth existence, he knows you have a child, he said I love children that's no disaster, look I brought you his picture, what do you think? I laughed, I kissed him: You're completely mad, darling father, besides he's not as good-looking as all that.

I wasn't able to turn down the invitation, so I went to the wedding thinking to please him. It was a Saturday evening. We parked the Peugeot in a vast parking lot and went in to the party. The music was much too loud, we faced a mass of lace, cleavage, sequins, jewelry, children running between the tables, little girls and old ladies trying to belly dance, everybody laughing; I felt out of place, wished I were somewhere else. Everything had been planned down to the last detail: the sequence of bands and shows, the menu, the wines, the merriment, and the surprises, all preannounced upon our arrival. On the program, then: a far-east ensemble and a big band, mini *brik* pastries, vol-au-vents, multitiered cakes, raspberry sorbets, stacks of cigar pastries in honey, strawberries with Chantilly, a grand chaos that amply told the story of such families still living with one foot in France and the other in Tunisia. Sitting at our table we found a very shy and very elegant man who stood to kiss my hand, his name was René, he was maybe the only person in that entire party who had anything in common with me. We didn't talk much, I drank two glasses of wine so I could breathe more easily and then I talked about anything and everything; at the head of the table, my father couldn't tell if we were getting along well, he watched us from his seat, worrying, I so loved the expressions in his questioning eyes, I made a little face to reassure him.

I remember that at one point I told the gentleman about *Pandora*, I'd seen it that afternoon at the Cinémathèque, I described to him the scene in which Ava Gardner asks her lover if, to prove his love, he would be ready to let his beautiful race car, which has taken him months to build, be driven off a cliff. She is frightening, that woman, beautiful but frightening, my mother used to adore her, she talked about her all the time, have you seen the film? The man looked at me strangely and, smiling, said no, no, I haven't much time for the cinema, the hospital consumes my waking hours. We didn't stay to the end of the party, I said he must excuse me but I had to go home, J-B was waiting for me and I still had reading to get through. My father stood and said all right all right, we'll be off, he looked down while taking leave of our table and by a dip of the chin indicated that he was obliged to follow me. I kissed my gentleman goodbye nicely, saying that I'd been delighted to make his acquaintance, and we left, weaving our way through the hubbub and the bunting. As we stepped outside, my father said he'd tried but he wouldn't push me, if I hadn't clicked with this man, he wouldn't mention it again, but there you go, he's a good option nonetheless, don't you think? I replied that of course it was no problem at all, the evening had been fun in any case, a little folksy, but no matter, and it had been a wonderful surprise to find Raoul Journo there, that alone made going worthwhile, when I think that he was at your wedding and he sang the very same song for you, it's crazy, what a fabulous voice he has, I almost wept you know, it took me back.

He was looking harried, he wasn't really listening, he kept craning right and left, I thought it was because of this business of failed marriages but it wasn't that, the problem was that he couldn't see his cherished Peugeot: But where did I put it, where did I put it, there are so many cars in

Paris, I'm going mad, I can't see it, what are we going to do? He also muttered a few words of Arabic that meant exactly the same: What shall we do, what shall we do? For a moment, I saw him again banging his head against the patio wall, beneath *The Card Players*. We looked all over the parking lot, and indeed the cars all looked the same, it was impossible to find our car. My father had his hand to his chest, I was very alarmed because he'd already had a scare a few months before and had been two days in intensive care in Hôpital Tenon. I told him not to worry, everybody loses their car sometimes, and especially in the hustle of a Saturday evening; we'd come back quite relaxed tomorrow morning and for now we'd simply take a taxi home, look, that one's free, come quickly, it's ours.

I often rerun that night, I know I sorely disappointed him but it couldn't be helped, I was not going to screw up my life to please him, and anyway, he seemed to have understood that. On the way home, he said, you did the right thing, go on with your life, only you know what you have to do, not I, I've always let you choose for yourself, I have confidence in you, and if you like, come with me tomorrow to look for the car?

A month had passed and now my father had something very important to tell me. I served him coffee with a slice of pistachio *pain de Gênes* that I'd made, his favorite cake. There was an elated urgency to his voice. I have to tell you what's happened to me, you won't believe it. Yesterday he'd had a "sensational" dream—that was another adjective he'd always loved. A film, a song, a woman, an ice cream, a dish of spaghetti, anything could be "sensational." I was keen to find out, go on, tell me your dream. In the ten years he'd been in Paris, I hadn't really seen him recapture his pleasure in life, he'd grown serious and anxious, he made fewer jokes, but that day his face was radiant once more. It's wonderful, for the first time I dreamed about the shop. Yes, about the shop, my shop, on Avenue de Carthage, it had my name on it, the yellow Machines Agricoles sign was there with the telephone number, 21–15–46, just below, my car was even parked outside, it was a dream but I thought it was real, I really had my shop back again, I was so happy! Such light in his eyes, such happiness.

Nothing had moved, the tractors, the combine harvesters, the spare parts, Ahmed, Stioui, and even Hossein the guard who smoked hash all day, he'd seen them all again, experienced it all. Everything was real life, I swear it's true, I swear I thought I was back there, that I'd never left. But how do dreams work? Can you explain? You could see the colors of the machines just perfectly, it was hot, I was in my yellow shirt and was chatting and joking with the workers. When I woke up, my eyes were wet. Do you think I wept in my dream, perhaps? I didn't know you could see all that at night, he kept saying, I didn't know that. I wanted to tell you straight away because I was afraid I'd forget.

It was ten years since he'd left Tunisia and given the shop to his workers, who were broadly stunned by his gesture. One morning, he'd brought them together and said look, I'm leaving for France and I'm entrusting the shop to you. Never forget that this is my life I'm trusting you with, now everything is yours, I don't wish to sell it, I prefer to give it to you. He never spoke again of the life we'd had, he faced each Parisian day as if it bore no relation to any of the others, he'd found his way, he managed to avoid feeling too much pain, at least so it appeared. He was no longer either joyful or sad, only dignified and always very elegant, he stood straight and wore perfectly cut suits. That day, he seemed to have a new flush of life, as if he were thirty again and life was starting anew, his voice was luminous, I think that's the best word for it. I asked him if he might want to go back to Tunisia for a few days, just to see his shop again for real and also to see our house once more, I could go with him, rent a place in Sidi-Bou-Saïd perhaps, we'd stay just three days and see how it felt. Hmm? He didn't answer, he could not answer. He only asked if he could have another small slice of cake, it's beautifully baked, *bravo*.

Besides, he never mentioned his dream ever again. He died two years later.

The boxes of spare parts lie around on the ground, to the left of the shop, you have to work your way through the sparks and the roar of the blowtorch to reach them. The reek of gasoline and rust, the smell of old machines in need of repair. The boxes are full of bolts, screws, cranks, cylinders, joints, axles; full of iron, steel, and cast-iron sections. They're stacked between my father's office and the great wasteland where the tractors and combine harvesters hold court out in the midday glare. For me, sitting in one of those huge tractors transports me straight to the countryside and to journeys up and down the land; my father crisscrosses Tunisia to meet his clients and, through him, I know the names of all the inland towns, I've always known them. I sit ready at the wheel and say them all aloud: Makthar, Thuburbo Majus, Enfidaville, Siliana, Grombalia, Le Kef, Kasserine, Sidi Bouzid. Men journey great distances in order to rummage in these boxes with both hands, they seem to know the purpose of every object, they scrutinize, consider, turn each object around and over, keep or reject it; all I see is rusty junk, I prefer to loiter in my father's office while he taps on his old typewriter, a great shiny black entity that fascinates and attracts me. I watch him tapping away at top speed at the wide keys, their stems rising in ripples, each letter's click is deafening, then suddenly to reach the next line the whole keyboard lifts and shifts over, the paper winds on, the text progresses, I see it unfurling down the other side of the ink bobbin, the letters are still shining wet and their smell permeates the office. On the shelves, files with the names of towns, and a few bolts, truants from the boxes outside. The moment my father steps out of the office, I race to take his place and try to do as he does, I'm six or seven years old, I take a fabulously white sheet of paper and slip it into the machine. Along the very top of each sheet is his name, in black print; I am proud of him, I want to learn to type so I can grow up to be like him. For I can quite see that, in those moments when he sits at his machine and his fingers are racing over the keyboard amid a gigantic clamor rivaling that of the fire-breathing blowtorches, yes, I do see that he is the writer here.

I must say again, before I finish this book, that for a long time, as a child and adolescent, I lived in fear. Everywhere, too many silent glances warning that some accident was close at hand. It wasn't very clear but the violence or disaster seemed imminent. I didn't know it was fear—I realized much later—but this nameless thing overwhelmed me, besieged me, submerged me, held me hostage. Ungraspable, it never left my side. Fear of the unspeaking faces that I encountered in the street, fear of an invisible violence that I sensed clearly but to which I could give no words. This was my inner experience, this was what shaped me, what I grew up on. I was a nervous child, I felt like an orphan even while my parents surrounded me with the best they could provide, I think it was their fragility that made me so nervous, the fragility in which they'd been mired from birth and perhaps even long before. They seemed so hapless, with no understanding of their own lives or of life itself, at all. And then there was the city. The battered sidewalks, the window bars on dilapidated buildings that were never repaired, the whitewash that peeled off in great flakes during the winter, the doors swollen with moisture, the strange skin diseases we saw on passers-by, leprosy, smallpox, bonnets worn to cover lice infestations, the torn dress of the enormous beggar woman on the synagogue steps, surrounded by her great baskets and her dazzlingly white dog for which she knitted multicolored coats; that's all she did: he was well dressed while she was in rags. All of this was strange and did not match up with my schoolbooks in which the poems and great texts bestrode the centuries, marked and measured them: each era had its own language and each of them was stunning, astonishing, the paper smelled so good, I wanted to sink into them, I wanted to be of books, and far from what I saw all around me. Even the synagogue felt incongruous on the Avenue de Paris: it was huge. I pretended to be a very happy child so I'd pass unnoticed and, more than anything, so as not to spread my fear in a home already teetering in fragile equilibrium.

I went on like that, saying nothing, making out it was fine. In any case, a great task awaited me: I had first of all to mend my parents, to darn their holes, heal their wounds, organize their lives, but how to go about this? So today I'm holding my baby father in my arms—this is what I've done all my life: cradle him, cradle them both in their innocence and sweetness, and even cradle what I call the country, never knowing exactly what I mean by the term. Tunisia or the long-past memories of my parents? I don't know. I held them up so they would not collapse. I chose reading to help me discover the best way of going about this. I chose pleasure. I chose love. Sensations, stories, shades of meaning. Now I think I got it all wrong. I should have been harder, sharper, more violent. I should have fought some other way. But that's how it was: every time I was transfixed by the

modest attentions of the people I met, by the delicacy of
a gesture or by the extraordinary way a life was retold, the
crucial detail dropped in at precisely the right moment; every time the laughter united and strengthened us, you have
to come here to understand and to love the very humblest
intimately for they are magnificent. And then there was the
balmy wind, the kiss of the air, the pale colors, the blue,
white, gray, and all this beauty of the sea right out to the
horizon, the movement of the skies that followed one after another, ever renewed, these helped me to camouflage
the tensions and the charged, sometimes jealous or malevolent looks—yes, we had those too. Still, I should have
gone about it differently. For example, the day Fadel invited
me for dinner with him, at his lovely villa near the steps, I
should have talked more, not let myself be overtaken by fear,
not pretended that I'd seen nothing. That day I nearly decided never to come back at all for just then there were also
Youssef's words when he suddenly turned very religious and
would no longer shake his friends' hands—Youssef whom
we used to call "the village prince." One morning, at the
market, he tossed me this strange question, when I'd just
come to stay for a few days, his eyes keen, sneering, hos-
tile, a filthy smile, he was unrecognizable: Why do you keep
coming back here? Aren't there other, prettier countries to
see than around here? Greece, for instance, don't you like
Greece, why don't you go to Greece? No point your coming
back here again and again. I couldn't reply, I was stricken.
If his words had been a silenced gun, I would have toppled,
there in the street, before the crates of oranges.

Fadel was Palestinian, he was living in Washington
where his parents had emigrated in 1948, completing a

degree in architecture and, for the past two years, going back and forth between Tunisia and the United States; it was the time when Arafat had the PLO headquarters set up in Tunis. Fadel was in love with Dominique Lehmann, she had left Paris abruptly and come back to live in Carthage, her living room looked over the ruins, close to the old Bey's Palladium, a rather tacky nightclub that had been very fashionable and that we used to call Zero for Conduct, as it had become notorious toward the end of the sixties for sex scandals involving several politicians. Dominique and Fadel had been living together for a few months and he had just discovered that she'd committed suicide. I was distraught, as was he; I'd gone for a walk with her in the Tunis medina a few days earlier, she'd bought an antique waistcoat covered in embroidery and encrusted with silver inlay, and I'd thought her so sparkling, so brave, perhaps a little overwrought, but I hadn't realized that she was feeling so lost. It was Fadel who told me, he loved her genuinely, and for his people it was unconscionable for him to be in love with a Jewess, yet he was unafraid, he loved her, he would always love her, an exceptional woman, he called her. We often had tea on his patio and we would talk of Dominique. He also showed me the plans for his project to rebuild the Little Sicily quarter in La Goulette. I was fascinated by his dedication; he wanted to restore the historic memory of this neighborhood and, in doing so, to restore old memories of the sympathy that used to exist between its several communities. We were carried away, we felt it was still possible, we told each other we would make it happen. One evening, then, he suggested I come by for dinner, he'd warned me that he had friends staying, but that's no problem, he'd added. It was not yet dark when I arrived, he introduced me to his two friends, they didn't shake my hand, just looked at me, looked me straight in the eyes, then went back inside. Fadel explained that they didn't speak French, they were Palestinians from Gaza. Don't worry, they've actually prepared everything for you, they didn't want any help from me, they know who you are, it's quite okay. The two men came back out, they laid newspaper over the low table in place of table linen, they brought out the big couscous and the four of us began to eat. In silence. Fadel was uneasy, he sensed my nervousness, I kept trying to talk but every sentence rang false, amid carrots and couscous I lost my appetite. The two men sat upright and, ignoring me, ate slowly, staring at the sky above the terrace. Night fell, no one turned the lights on.

It was then that I thought I might have walked into a trap, that perhaps they were going to kill me.

Don't you have any lights?

Yes, Fadel said, but they don't like electric lights, they prefer to stay in the dark, it's what they're used to, don't worry, luckily we have a fine moon this evening. Now, won't you have some more chickpeas? I said no, thanks, I had some work still to do, I had to go back. I wasn't sure I'd make it to the door, my heart was beating so hard, panic had taken over, but I was polite right to the end. My lips were trembling, yet they managed a smile. The two men cleared their plates as soon as they'd finished their last mouthfuls, they brought a basket of oranges, they did not say goodbye to me, they left me alone with Fadel. He said again that they'd prepared everything for me but they were shy, that's all, you see they even left in order not to disturb us. I said that the couscous was excellent and would he thank them for me, but I would rather go back. The garden was pitch black. Fadel, like a gentleman, would walk with me as far as the Hôtel du Figuier but first we stopped at the Café des Nattes for a verbena tea, this was our ritual. There was a little *ma'luf* band in the middle of the café, the space had become their stage, and we the audience settled all around, reclining on mats. As we stepped inside, amid the scent of the *shishas*, I recognized "Ya Chouchana," a favorite song and one I often listened to in Paris; Oulaya's voice and the male singers accompanying her instantly recalled Tunisia's colors, I wanted to go back to them; this song, and those of Raoul Journo, Feyrouz, Umm Kulthum, and Farid al-Atrash, were part of me. But that evening I was completely dislocated, a sudden, crushing discouragement. Luckily I was due back in Paris the following morning and I completely wrote off that strange evening, I wiped it from my life. I never told anyone about it. Wiped out until this evening when it came back, the whole story, on the terrace of this house in Sidi-Bou-Saïd, in this book that I mean to finish before daybreak, as a farewell gesture to the country.

I remember it all. After writing the book's last words, I went out onto the terrace, the sun was showing red at the far edge of the sea, soon it would be fully risen, another scorching day in the making. I knew that in a few minutes it would reach the little whitewashed bench. I brewed some coffee and sat there, as I did every morning. I took a photo and posted it on Facebook, on my wall, with these words: "A last one before the road." I'd gotten into the habit of posting a photo of the same blue window of sea, taken from the little white bench, under the ever-changing light and skies, in all seasons. I lowered the blinds, the taxi was already outside, I recognized its engine, Ridah always kept good time, we kissed goodbye. The airport was practically deserted, flights must have been canceled, the freshly washed tiles, I stared at the words Tunis-Carthage, seeing them as if for the first time, they were practically abandoned. In a state of readiness but still smiling, police were trying to reassure the few passengers: Don't worry, *bon voyage*, see you again soon. Inside the plane, I dozed, plugged in to my music, my twenty-five most listened-to tracks: Pavarotti, Feyrouz, Bashung, Barbarina's aria, Hindi Zahra, Vivaldi's *Stabat Mater*, Raúl Paz. It was a fine day, I'd left the furnace behind, the captain announced that we would be reaching Paris in two hours and twenty minutes, I began to breathe more freely, I thought of Alain on his boat, that was sixteen days ago now, again I saw his head slumped on the guardrail, his lips whispering, "We'll go on," the Amorgos coast growing farther away, the forest of Gammarth where he had been buried, I had no desire to be cut off from his presence, from his last words, I too wanted to go on, to go on for him, and I wondered if ultimately his death had not indeed been connected, indirectly, to that decision to stop writing. He would never have gone out to sea like that, a self-made exile from himself: this had killed him. No, I had no right, this was stupid, his death would remain our mystery, one day it might be illuminated. This is what I was thinking in that plane flying me back to Paris. I thought of the Lully aria he had listened to with J-B the night before his death. *Atys*: his favorite opera. They'd been on the bridge, after dinner, and in silence, in the darkness, they had followed the trajectory of Atys's sleep, of his dreams that lifted the heart, "pleasant dreams" as the libretto called them. *Atys*—the first tragedy in which the hero dies on stage. The music rang out over the sea, and something intimate formed between Alain and J-B just then, a kind of friendship pact, a brotherhood. The image of Alain on his yacht is overlaid by Flaubert's famous words, written in Croisset to Louise Colet, one Saturday night in 1853. In this letter he's describing the doubts that regularly assailed him while he wrote, and his slowness, the amount of work he still has to do. "Oh benighted profession! Oh damned obsession! Yet we sing its praises, our treasured torment. Without it we die. Life is tolerable only on condition of never being in it." And the music swelled, I wanted it to shape this last journey by infusing it with joy, I let it work on me, let it flood through me. Each voice was a photo, in a thousand and one dimensions. First a close-up, with all the nuances, the cherished expressions, then subtly details started to appear in the background, the voice grew plainer, bare, it showed me visions and hearts hidden in the depths of each syllable, there were blood and joy, strength and fragility, and again I saw behind the voice, beyond it, the outskirts of cities, rumpled sheets, a glorious confidence in life, hearts answering each other and proliferating, their growing magnetic attraction, I knew the minutest nuances in each of them, I remembered all of it, I was creating it, my little love factory was working again at last, in the midst of the clouds. I was serene, I'd stopped thinking about the radical move I had just made: departing, leaving what I most loved. Suddenly a man came and slumped down on me, he laid his head on my shoulder like a child and very calmly said: Nobody loves me, my children don't love me anymore, my wife doesn't love me, they've had enough of me, so I've come to sit here beside you, at least I'm okay here. I lowered the volume of my headphones. Behind us, his three children, about thirteen, ten, and five years old, were in fits. Behind them, his very pretty wife was holding a baby in her arms dressed in blue, doubtless it was a boy. She must have bought the children sandwiches and Cokes, for the stewardess now leaned over the man who was still pressed against my shoulder, his eyes tightly closed, eyelids quivering a little, it was clear he wasn't asleep, he was pretending, he'd simply had enough. She tapped on his arm as stewardesses do when they have to wake a passenger, with great delicacy, and she repeated for the third time: *Monsieur*, please, your wife has no money, she says it's you who should pay. No, I'm not paying, the man said without opening his eyes, I don't care, I'm not paying. The children began to drum their knees on the seats in front, *Papa*, *Papa*, you have to pay, we bought things. I'll come back later, the stewardess said, I'll serve the other passengers, you can speak to your wife. The three children repeated in unison *Papa*, *Papa*, we were hungry, you have to pay, she'll pay you back in Paris. And he unmoved. I hiding my laughter in my hands. Give it all back, I don't care, pretend I'm not here. And once more he tucked his head against my shoulder, to huddle like a small kid. The children told him it was too late, they'd already eaten everything, they couldn't give anything back. They were laughing and trying to convince me I shouldn't worry, he'd end up paying, they were used to this, he was a lovely father and always let them have their way, he just did a bit of play-acting sometimes that's all. In the end, the man handed a note to the children without looking at them and said to me you see how weak I am, my whole life it's been like this, pushover that I've become. Last week, they wanted to see the Eiffel Tower and go to France because they were too hot, I said okay and I bought the tickets, we're going to stay with my brother who lives in the 20th arrondissement, I'm always trying to make them happy even if I haven't got much money, the problem is that of course I get tired, my country tires me, my family tires me, the baby's exhausting but I love them, I can't help it, that's life, that's how it is… I asked him which town they were from. Nabeul, he replied. And of course we talked about the attacks, he no longer recognized his country, the young man a Tunisian, it was unthinkable, we could never have imagined this would happen to us.

I guarded Alain's smile inside me, very gentle, his death had been such a straightforward death, so simple. I put Chavela Vargas on again, a little louder. "Somos." A decadent song, perfect for this journey through the sky. *Somos un sueño imposible, que busca la noche.* Her old woman's voice, her face where the wrinkles had become a kind of writing, a landscape. In the log for his first voyage in the yacht, Alain had remarked: "The fact of having stopped writing has become like an obsession. The lack is there, flagrant, irremediable, without remedy. The imperatives of navigation are such that I hope: even if I don't start writing again, I should, in all this time, at least be able to take stock. Meanwhile latitudes and longitudes will be penciled onto the map to show where we are and if this milestone is still the right one—within myself, too. For I must admit that, since I stopped writing, I've been somewhat adrift. I have lost my bearings and no longer know which shore to call home. Writing is a froth that leaves no trace of any plough." Ahead of me, a baby was crying, she was a little girl between six and nine months old, in a sleeveless white dress. From between the seats, I watched her father hold her close in his arms and whisper very softly, to soothe her, the prayer I used to hear regularly through the mosques' loudspeakers; I recognized the words, I listened hard to be sure I wasn't mistaken but no, it was indeed that prayer. The little girl's hair was shiny and already very curly, her father's voice had lulled her to sleep.

I looked through the last photos that I'd taken on my phone. After the one of the sunrise, there was Noah's Ark, the little painting on glass that hung in the bedroom, opposite the window. I looked at that one for a long time, thinking that, by writing this book, I too had shipped away with me all that I loved and wanted to save. In fact, this was my fight for softness. Instead of animals and birds, I had stowed my parents' radiant faces and the small town of Ariana—that had been the guiding thread to my labyrinth; upon these I had laid the colors of La Marsa and of the whole country, I had packed the past few centuries, wedding carpets, the terra-cotta vase, grandfather's fabrics and jewelry, the music and words of Mathilde, Souad, Slim, Fadel, Dominique, Kriss, Jacques, and Alain, I hugged them tightly to me, I would not leave them. Standing on the boat, by the sails, were Madame Henry and Julien, tall Lucie and José, Frank and Fernand Delalande, the cows asleep in the neighboring field and of course a few spare parts for tractors and combine harvesters that would have been too heavy for the journey: without these I couldn't have reconstructed anything. The rainbow and the dove, these too I acknowledged, as I acknowledged Bazou and Rio Bravo. Cabin crew: doors to manual and cross-check—I was relieved, we'd arrived in Paris and the temperature was thirty degrees. Take care, said the captain, laughing: Reports are that winds from the Sahara are going to sweep the country starting Tuesday, get ready for a real heat wave.

Months have passed, more than a year now.

The only thing I forgot to say is that at the last minute, posting the sunrise photo on Facebook, I deleted the caption I first wrote for it, "A last one before the road," and replaced it with this: "Always returning."

I stared at that photo for a long time, then I pressed the button on the remote to lower the blinds and closed the door.

I knew I could not do it—I couldn't help it, I would always be returning.